Dear Father Peter
Forty-nine Years of Letters to a Priest

The Reverend Canon Peter Gwillim Kreitler

Foreword by the Reverend J. Barney Hawkins IV, PhD

VTS PRESS

Copyright © 2019 by The Reverend Canon Peter Gwillim Kreitler

All rights reserved. No part of this book may be reproduced, stored in a retrieval system, or transmitted in any form or by any means, electronic or mechanical, including photocopying, recording, or otherwise, without the written permission of the publisher.

First Published in the United States by

VTS Press
Virginia Theological Seminary
3737 Seminary Road
Alexandria, VA 22304
www.vts.edu

ISBN: 978-0-578-57239-0

Printed in the United States of America

FIRST EDITION

Cover design by Megan Sheets

I dedicate *Dear Father Peter* to my three grandchildren, Theo, Belle, and Megan, and to the children and grandchildren throughout the world who will be challenged by the indifference—most especially to the collapsing of creation—shown by so many in positions of power. In so dedicating these forty-nine years of letters, I also encourage my grandchildren and young people everywhere to write letters to politicians, business leaders, and other agents of change to express their concerns for their future and the future of their children.

Foreword

We often refer to priests by the role they are playing. Priests' roles as leader and administrator are expressed by titles such as rector, vicar, and parish associate. The words curate and pastor remind us of the priest as caregiver. There is priest as theologian, preacher, and educator. In celebrations of the Holy Eucharist, the priest is referred to as presider or celebrant. Often, the priest is known as preacher. In our book *Staying One, Remaining Open: Educating Leaders for a 21st Century Church*, my colleagues and I profile individuals who, like Peter Kreitler, expand the scope of ministry. In Peter's case, his call to care for God's creation—a preoccupation of his since the first Earth Day in 1970—was so strong that he left his decades-long parish ministry to establish a non-profit organization to advocate and teach on behalf of our planet.

In this remarkable collection of more than 150 letters, we gain insight into the diverse and fulfilling career of this twentieth-century servant leader. There is Peter, riding forty hours on a bus with the youth group on their way to one of several mission trips in Mexico. There is the priest with a flair for experiential learning, producing a multimedia exhibit depicting the trash that was piling up on his local beaches and building a Noah's ark out of twelve thousand bottle corks to teach about climate change and sea level rise. And here he is, working with ex-convicts and gang members to clean up graffiti. As surely as he has a voice for this "fragile earth, our island home," we also see that Peter has a heart for human relationships, which are equally fragile. Deeply empathetic, the joys of those he meets are Peter's joys and the sadness of others become his care. Rather than pretending to know it all though, he also shares several pastoral challenges that were "above his paygrade" and stresses that priests should acknowledge their own limitations in training and ability. He makes a strong case for each of us to grant others a second chance and be welcoming when someone stumbles. Echoing the shortest letter in the compilation—"Apology accepted"—Peter accepts others as he does himself, flaws and all.

We see Peter as both teacher and disciple and identify with many of the experiences that helped him grow. Writers as young as seven and as mature as ninety—and every age in between—challenge and encourage him and, in some cases, offer advice that is as memorable as it is direct and effectual. Who could ignore the counsel to "keep a tan all year long and don't smoke dope, it will ruin your career"? In a time when more and more people are relying on digital communications, Peter cherishes his family's tradition of putting pen to paper. Whether the letters are crayon-embossed or on the letterhead of a celebrity or an elected official, they are mirrors that reflect Peter's ministry and the joy, humor, and pathos of the human condition.

Caregiver. Environmental warrior. Creative teacher. Life-long learner. Peter Kreitler is a rare breed. As a priest of The Episcopal Church for "only" thirty-nine years, I commend Peter who, in his late seventies, still exercises his environmental and pastoral ministry. I believe this book will have a lasting impact; his letters will inspire this generation and coming generations of church leaders—both lay and ordained. Just as we see God's fingerprints all over Peter's multi-colored robe of service, the pages you are about to read speak to the God-touched spark in all of us. *Dear Father Peter* asks us all, What colors will your personal ministry take? What gifts will you offer to the world?

---J. Barney Hawkins, IV

The Reverend J. Barney Hawkins IV, PhD retired from Virginia Theological Seminary in 2017 as Vice President for Institutional Advancement and the Arthur Carl Lichtenberger Professor of Pastoral Theology and now serves as co-director of the Bicentennial Campaign.

The Story Begins

I was born during the Second World War. My mom and I lived with both sets of my grandparents for the first few years of my life while my dad was in the Navy, flying seaplanes along the Eastern Seaboard looking for German U-Boats. During the early 1940s, my family members communicated long distance via handwritten letters—with one exception. When Mom went off to college in 1934, her father, Stanley Sessions "Pop" Gwillim, dictated letters to his secretary to type and send to her at Wheaton College. Almost eighty years later, I was going through family archives stored at my grandparents' home on Cape Cod, Massachusetts and came across a stack of thirty-two well-preserved letters from my grandfather to my mom. They are a treasure trove of a father's counsel, advice, and encouragement to a daughter he loved. I had been saving the correspondence that I received since my ordination to the priesthood in 1970, but the significance of these two tales of archived letters was not apparent until one night when my wife Katy and I were having dinner with her parents. The subject of writing letters came up and my mother-in-law, Nanny Bates, blurted out, "I like letters because I can read them over and over again, and when you are older you forget phone conversations!"

I started to rethink the value of the letters that I had been saving and, rather unceremoniously, tossing into shoe boxes. I decided to use the downtime during my cancer treatments to read and sort several hundred of the letters. To my delight, I found that the letters are wonderfully varied, with content ranging from the profound to the silly, and authors ranging from the humble to the most exalted. Many of the letters are signed, others are not, and I have withheld several names in the letters that address sensitive or confidential matters.

While the letter writers range from grade-school students to presidents of the United States, none of them stands higher or lower on my ladder of esteem. Not one letter in *Dear Father Peter* is more important than another because each message addresses an aspect of my life and offers valuable information. In fact, the sentiments the writers expressed—whether critical or laudatory—shaped who I am and who I am becoming to this day. These letters capture the essence of what Paul Tillich—a theologian whose systematics baffled me during my seminary years—meant when he described our journeys through life as "being is becoming." In order to become more fully human, we must always be on the path of becoming more loving, more understanding, and more accepting. Well into my eighth decade of life, the letters remind me that I will always be a disciple—a learner—and will always be grateful that many different people took the time to write me with such candor.

First typewriters, and later computers and social media, have all but obliterated the practice of communicating via handwritten letters. For those who are wedded to digital communication, I would caution you to save emails or text messages for posterity. As I have reread countless personal letters, I have realized that the messages they contain are just as fresh and relevant as the day they were written.

I begin with three letters that set the context for the rest of *Dear Father Peter*. The first is a letter from Pop to Mom in 1934. The second is a letter that my paternal grandparents wrote me in 1943, when I was just one year old. The third is from the rector[1] of my childhood church, Christ Church, Short Hills New Jersey, who wrote me in 1953 when I was eleven. My hope is that *Dear Father Peter* will inspire others to continue the generational gift of letter writing that I received from my family.

---

[1] The rector is the clergy boss of a parish.

October 12, 1934 *...I am, therefore, recommending to you that you bear in mind the importance of the following three characteristics...good health, character, and judgment.*

    Stanley Sessions Gwillim

July 17, 1943 *When you arrived on July 21, 1942, you were a messenger who carried with him a great deal of joy and happiness.*

    Nanny and Poppy Kreitler

December 23, 1953 *Last night I heard you read the scriptural account of the birth of our Lord and I want to congratulate you on the wonderful rendition you made of it.*

    The Reverend Herbert H. Cooper

October 12, 1934

As I look back on my prep school and college years, it seems to me that during those years I formed habits and developed characteristics that followed me through the rest of my life. I am, therefore, recommending to you that you bear in mind the importance of the following three characteristics, which start to be developed during your present prime of life. These characteristics are good health, character, and judgment.

In the matter of good health, it is quite easy to forget the necessity for being reasonably careful in your habits, to obtain a reasonable amount of sleep, to eat the right kind and right amount of foods, and to take a sufficient amount of exercise to keep your body in healthy condition.

At your age and for the next few years you will, if you live right, develop your physical condition to such a degree that it will be of great benefit to you in later years. With a good foundation built up during the growing years, much less worry about poor health is apt to follow in later years. This is your individual responsibility, and it should be given a reasonable amount of consideration as you go along in life.

In the matter of character, these are the formative years, and if in your dealings with others you are always fair and honest, it is quite likely that you will always hold the respect of your associates, for it will be [one] of the most valuable assets, and a good character is built up only by applying some effort to its development. A person whose word cannot be depended upon and who is not fair-minded cannot be considered as having an admirable character. There is nothing more important than to have the reputation of being a person of good character.

In the matter of judgment, this is acquired by experience and is not something that a person possesses all of a sudden. It is developed by a reasonable amount of thinking being applied to the task at hand, and it is only by exercising your thinking powers that judgment is developed. Before committing yourself to a debatable point or to the answer to any important problem, it is well to review the pros and cons before arriving at your decision and, if you do this, it should develop in you a reasonable amount of good judgment, which will be a great asset to you in later life.

Love, Dad

I wish I had known about these letters during my formative years. My maternal grandfather's advice would have been a strong foundation on which to build.

Our Dear Grandson Peter,   **July 17, 1943**

When you arrived on July 21, 1942, you were a messenger who carried with him a great deal of joy and happiness. To your grandparents Gwillim and Kreitler you brought the happiness that always accompanies the first grandson. And during this first year of your stay with us you have brought cheer and contentment and gladness into all our homes.

On your first birthday I want you to have a gift that you can remember for a long while. I am, therefore, sending you three hundred U.S. Series E war bonds. These will mature when you are eleven years old [and also] when you are at school and when you can probably use them to very good advantage.

You are too young now to understand the reason for the purchase of the war bonds or to understand the deep love which goes with this gift, but as you grow up, your Mommy and your Daddy will explain these and many other questionable things to you.

Lots and Lots of Love,

    From, Nanny and Poppy Kreitler

I didn't know anything about this letter until I discovered it in my parents' archives in the summer of 2018. Along with the letters that my maternal grandfather wrote to my mom, it confirms the importance of letter writing in our family. I am sure that Leonora and John Kreitler—Nanny and Poppy to me—sent me my first piece of mail, as it arrived in time for my first birthday. What makes it special to me is that their reference to "this first year of your stay with us" confirms that all four of my grandparents had a hand in raising me during my first four years of life. I was so fortunate to begin life in a loving family. Our relationships during our early years have a profound effect on the people we become, and I know that my family provided a strong foundation on which to build the rest of my life. For that reason, I always stress with couples whom I counsel or marry that they take time to understand their life scripts by having honest discussions about each other's family histories and dynamics. It is often fun, and always enlightening, to learn about one another's families.

December 23, 1953

Christ Church in Short Hills

Dear Peter,

Last night I heard you read the scriptural account of the birth of our Lord and I want to congratulate you on the wonderful rendition you made of it. It was done beautifully, reverently, and with real meaning. Congratulations and good luck!

A merry Christmas and a happy, peaceful New Year to you all.

> *Sincerely,*
>
> *Herbert H. Cooper*

Here we are at just the third letter in the book—written seventeen years prior to my ordination—and we've set the stage for what was to come later in my life.

The Reverend Herbert Hannan Cooper was the rector of Christ Church Short Hills, the church that I attended when I was growing up in New Jersey. He wrote me this congratulatory missive when I was just eleven years old. This is my first piece of correspondence from a member of the clergy. To this day, I take pride in elocution, especially from the pulpit. Reading well allows our congregants to hear the Word more clearly. The best presentation of scripture that I ever heard was when Charlton Heston read at our church; without exception our parishioners hung on his every word. My paternal grandmother, Nanny, always remarked that she took something away from every sermon she heard—and living until ninety meant that she heard a lot of sermons.

An adult "person of the cloth" taking the time to write to an eleven-year-old sets the bar high for all of our letter-writing efforts. Here we are, more than six decades later, reading this emboldening and encouraging letter. Of course, I was not a priest then, but who knows if my path was not paved with my grandparents' letter to me in 1943 and Reverend Cooper's letter in 1953? I cannot pinpoint one event—because it was actually a series of circumstances—that most likely propelled me towards ordination, but in these letters, I have rediscovered the signposts that marked the route on my way to being and becoming the person that I am.

It's a tough time to be a "liberal" Christian. Hang in.
Chaplain Charles Baldwin, Brown University

Charles Adams Baldwin
Office of the Chaplain
Brown University

Dear Peter,

You're a delight to write. God told me she had not called me to be a college, or any other kind of, president. Your other comment humbles, is totally without merit, and I love it.

Peter, I remember you well and with great fondness. I hope you and your ministry thrive. It's a tough time to be a "liberal" Christian. Hang in.

All the best,

Charlie

One of the greatest members of the church that I have ever known, the late Charlie Baldwin, was a Congregational minister, chaplain at Brown University from 1958 until 1988, and interim president of the historically black Tougaloo University—to name a few aspects of his fabled career. For me, he lived out the meaning of ecumenism, embraced the challenge of confronting social injustice, and demonstrated the power of proactive religion. He was the model of a modern person of the cloth. If he is the embodiment of a "liberal" Christian, sign me up.

Charles Baldwin walks with four other clergy whom I have known and admired: William Sloan Coffin, former Presiding Bishop John Hines, the Reverend Dr. George Regas, and Father Thomas Berry. May the light of these great individuals continue to shine brightly. As the first century Stoic philosopher Seneca wrote to his friend Lucilius, "There is a need, in my view, for someone [to serve] as a standard against which our characters can measure themselves."[2] I would be eternally humbled to have my name mentioned with Charlie's anytime; he and the men mentioned above are some of my heroes.

---

[2] Simon Dru, "The Power of Examples – What Stoics Say about Mentors and Examples," Rise to the Good Life, May 7 2016, www.risetothegoodlife.com/the-power-of-examples-what-stoics-say-about-mentors-and-examples.

Peter J. Kreitler   *5/31/71*

I urge that for the general good and welfare of St. Andrew's, you, without delay, submit your resignation to the vestry.[3]   Signed, G.H.

This letter delivered a real dose of reality about life in ministry. I was ordained to the Episcopal priesthood on April 27, 1970 under the watchful eye of Bishop Robert Spears of the Diocese of West Missouri. Just a little over a year later, I was beginning to figure out what I was supposed to be doing as the young minister on the block when, to my consternation, this letter showed up. Even before I read this individual's letter, I knew that I was in trouble. By that time, I was usually addressed as Father Peter, Reverend Kreitler, or just Peter. This salutation contained no title and the wrong middle initial separated my first and last names. By the time I had read his clear directive, I knew that ministry was going to be—at the least— interesting and most likely tough at times!

To this day I cannot recall why the gentleman was so upset with me, but the issue of my leaving the Kansas City parish of St. Andrew's escalated to a call for a vote to dismiss. Surprisingly, the vote to keep me on was unanimous. When my early detractor was asked why he did not vote to fire me, he answered, "When my wife was dying, Peter held my hand."

This elderly parishioner—a person of few words—became a friend. His twenty-one-word admonition and his subsequent comment influenced me early in my career and continues to shape my ministry to this day. This experience underscored for me that the most important facet of a priest's portrait is to be a pastor. "Caring for the flock" is not a cliché. Being present and showing up in the lives of our parishioners is the primary manifestation of what our ordination vows call us to be. There is truth in the saying "baptism by fire" and I have learned that slings and arrows will come as you follow your truth, attempt to live out the teachings of the Gospel, and mirror the behavior of Jesus of Nazareth. Yet this whole episode demonstrated that healing and growth can ensue if one remains steadfastly faithful to the task of being a priest. Remember, reconciliation with detractors is always possible. Over the past five decades I have tried to win over many individuals who have seen things differently than I do. Even when I could not change certain hearts and minds, there was still value in communicating and attempting to bridge the gap between us.

And with a degree of hubris, for the good of the parish, I did not resign.

---

[3] A vestry is the governing body of a local Episcopal congregation.

Dear Peter,   *10/7/71*

The following will probably not be a good job, but as I cannot dismiss from my mind the fairly lengthy tirade on what you thought the church was not doing last Tuesday, I felt that something should be said to you by somebody! As you finished it, I had to bite my tongue and keep myself from jumping up and yelling, "BULLSHIT–BALONEY! Peter Kreitler just doesn't know what the priesthood is all about; somebody has failed him and the church in his training." Well, I would still say the same thing but I do feel in retrospect that it wouldn't have done anything that day. I do feel that if a vote had been taken at that moment that your position would have received about 98 plus percent defeat; almost no one in that room would have agreed with your analysis of the church's job or action. Now this percentage might be off one way or the other (not much leeway at the top position), but it is damn near the truth. Now where does that leave you? It should certainly mean that you ought to find out what the priesthood is all about for one thing—the first thing—to be realistic, and then determine whether or not it is your vocation or not. I, for one, do not believe that everybody in that room is so dumb, so thickheaded, so obtuse, so recalcitrant, or so establishment that they cannot see the sickness of the day and are trying in their way in the priesthood to do something about it. I think it would behoove you at this point to thoroughly analyze your thinking position to see whether it is the church or you that needs a change of direction. I think that a goodly number of us (and I guess I must place myself to the fore as I speak primarily of and from my position) have just as many marbles as you do and in some case a hell of a lot more. Plus the fact that most of us have had about twenty-five years more experience with human nature than you. By stating this I am in no measure or in any sense trying to put you down, but it is the truth and unless we are so dumb that we can't see or read the handwriting on the wall, this experience should be of some merit in our lives and work. At your young age, you think that you know the answers and I for one think that you do not. Having known some young priests similar to yourself, I have some knowledge of the frustration you are undergoing; this frustration will never be resolved (if, indeed, it should ever be resolved) by trying to be a social worker under the guise of a priest of the church. Hopefully, one of these days we can get together for a personal chat re: the above. Lacordaire's enclosed "thou art a priest forever" has always been my ideal and guide in the priesthood; I'm sure that I have not always lived up to it but it is the best definition I have ever found. Faithfully…[Name Redacted]

Early in my career, I was criticized by some for speaking up for the marginalized LGBTQ community, God's collapsing creation, and a progressive agenda for the church. Ironically, this colleague left The Episcopal Church for a conservative diocese in Africa before we could have a personal chat.

January 29, 1973

Dear Peter,

Your dream speaks of the four, which is the great symbol of wholeness. This is the gift of the greatest price to you and you have to obey its laws. Those laws are not easy, but win the Kingdom for one. A pair of pairs is the finest symbol of the quaternity. The quaternity dissolves into another pair of pairs and leaves one extra. This is not an improvement and is not as durable as the quaternity. I wish I could speak for hours with you. There is so much to say about the man who has a chance at the quaternity and what is demanded of him. Stay with what you have, even if it means much suffering. When everything has burned that can burn—then one must be still. It is the place of miracles. Just stay quiet where you are. There is no other place for you to go.

Peace, strength,

Robert

Robert Johnson, author of the books *He, She,* and *We,* was a Jungian psychoanalyst who opened his Solana Beach, California home to me in in the spring of 1973. This modest home overlooking the Pacific Ocean was a spartan testimony to a deeply spiritual man who, on several occasions, offered counsel and advice to one just beginning his own personal journey. Being able to work with Robert to discern what dreams are all about was one of the many gifts he gave me.

The final paragraph of his eloquent letter of direction reminded me of a portion of the Old Testament's Psalm 37, "Be still before the Lord and wait patiently for Him." In our frenetic twenty-first century lives—fraught with illnesses that alter our paths, complex international policies that confuse, the ravages of climate change, and rising and falling economic indices—we are well advised to take a deep breath and be still. Staying quiet where we are can be a miraculous place of transformation or understanding. As another personal guide along my journey, Dr. John O'Hearne, counseled, "Peter, take ten minutes a day to restore your island quality." Mountains of advice have come my way, but "try being still, Peter" is a phrase I repeat on a regular basis.

Dear Father Kreitler,

I am a son of the first Indian to be a bishop of the Methodist Church, but it was his views that encouraged my search to include other religions as well as Christianity. This has widened my appreciation of Jesus and of the depth and wideness of his teachings. I would like to quote to you the words of Sai Baba, a holy man in India, whose teachings are almost identical with those of Jesus: "The Lord can be addressed by any Name that tastes sweet to your tongue, or pictured in any Form that appeals to your sense of wonder and awe. There is no need for you to change your religion and follow me after you have heard me. Follow the God of your choice in the manner familiar to you, and you will find that you are coming closer and closer to me. The cultivation of Love and Love alone will prove to man that there is only one religion, the religion of Love...and to only one God and He is Omnipresent. Let the different faiths exist. Let them flourish, and let the glory of God be sung in all the languages and in a variety of tunes. That should be the ideal. **Accept the different faiths and recognize them as valued so long as they do not extinguish the flame of unity."**

I. Amar Chitambar M.D.

When Dr. Chitambar wrote, he had no idea about my connection to his native country, language, and religions. My interest in the region began when I was a boy, listening to stories about my maternal great uncle Major General Alan Whiteside, who had been second in command of the Pakistan Army. He lived in Rawalpindi from 1918 until 1948, and, when he returned home to England, he taught Urdu to British civil servants. Ironically, it was the writings of another Methodist bishop, Chandu Ray of West Pakistan (1912-1983), that furthered my fascination with India and Pakistan. I wrote to Bishop Ray and told him about Uncle Alan and about my interest in coming to intern with him. In response, Bishop Ray wrote Bishop Anand of Amritsar, Punjab, India, who invited me to come work with the Anglican missionary Rev. Ken Coleman at the Christian Rural Training Center in Ajnala. I arrived in June of 1963, and my four months there had such an impact on me that when I returned to college, I studied Hinduism, read the Vedas and Upanishads, and studied Sanskrit. My time in rural India helped develop my theology and my understanding that we are all one family on this earth. More than thirty years after I received this stranger's letter, his powerful words resonate in my heart more strongly than ever. I abhor the vitriol thrown at those of different skin colors or religions. The wisdom of this seer from India helps foster "the flame of unity" so essential in our world today. Dr. Chitambar, if you ever read this, please get in touch. The beautiful prose you shared is filled with a lifetime of wisdom for a member of any faith.

October 5, 1975

Dear Peter,

Please, please forgive me for not answering sooner. I have no real excuses.

The fifteen years my family spent there helped me to grow a lot (still a lot of growing to do) and I rejoice that God was able to use me in bringing people into a deeper relationship with Him.

Perhaps I should mention that the letter you sent ended up in our Primate's office and he took time to find out to whom it was sent (only my first name) and then was kind enough to personally send it on to me.

Ken

I had written to the Reverend Ken Coleman to let him know about my ordination to the Episcopal priesthood. I was pleased to hear back from him because his mentoring, challenging style of interaction, and his deep commitment to the people he served during his fifteen-year missionary work in India was exemplary. I could write an entire book about my experience in India, but suffice it to say that Ken was the embodiment of what I thought a priest should be. I was indeed lucky to learn at his feet for four months, from June through September of 1963. Ken's family had moved to the hill country of the Himalayas in order to escape the summer heat, so Ken, his cook, and I were the only ones inhabiting the mission in Ajnala, Punjab India at the time. There I was, twenty years old, bicycling from village to village to watch Ken minister to his many mission outposts. I took every chance I could to absorb the grace and wisdom of this humble man. He once said to me over mutton, onion, and potatoes—our staple Anglicized food—"Feed the belly first, and then talk about the church and its teachings later." Another dinner-table gem of his was, "Peter, if you go into ministry, do not look for rewards. They will come, but don't look for them."

I have always thought of an enlightened person as being one who has a soft heart for all in God's creation. Ken was enlightenment personified. His light revealed a whole new path for me and still illuminates my journey today.

Dear Peter,

It will be very good to have you and a group of young people with us this coming summer. I have talked with Father Jose Tlaseca and he is most enthusiastic about having you all in Alejandra. The dates you mention are fine and, as you have been there before, you know about such things as clothing requirements.

As for the two-week clinic, the dentist should have no problems and he is certainly needed. We have a doctor here in the city who holds a once-a-month medical clinic in Alejandra and Ticuman, and she has testified often about the poor condition of the teeth. With my very best wishes and looking forward to seeing you again in Mexico, I remain

Sincerely yours,

Jose G. Saucedo

Bishop of Central and South Mexico

I had the opportunity to live and work in rural India and Mexico during two summers between years at Brown University. In 1970 I had the chance to give members of the St. Andrew's Youth Group a similarly eye-opening and life-enhancing experience by taking them on a mission trip to Mexico.

The warmth of the Mexican people instantly melted away any preconceptions that our forty sojourners may have had, and to see the youth of Kansas City playing with the children of Ticuman and Alejandra made all of us proud. One day we were invited to hike in our bathing suits to the springs. There, just fifteen minutes away from the villages, we discovered the most beautiful oasis of water and jungle. The cool spring water refreshed us all and the inner tube trip down the river lasted almost half an hour. The dental clinic was a big success; the villagers, who had never visited a dentist, would line up every day to receive our gifts of a toothbrush and toothpaste. Items that we take for granted, they appreciated as something special.

The youth group hosted three trips during my tenure in Kansas City and I know that to this day, almost fifty years later, the experience is fresh in everyone's memory. Thanks, Bishop Saucedo, for opening your heart and communities to us. We gained more than we gave, and will always cherish the generosity of spirit we found in rural Mexico. In retrospect, our two communities were breaking down barriers that had previously separated us. The privileged American youth and the Mexican young people worked together while respecting and honoring each other's differences. A life lesson for all of us, indeed—build bridges, not walls!

Dear Peter,

Project Mexico is one of the most rewarding, fulfilling experiences I have had in my life. The lessons I have learned by participating in this project are invaluable. I am very interested in plans to return to Mexico this year.

Sincerely, Elaine

Dear Peter,

I would like to participate in the Mexico project because I think I could grow by and enjoy having exposure to a foreign culture. It would also be testing grounds and good preparation for my future plans of Peace Corps or something similar when I graduate.

Sincerely, Becky

One of the most delightful aspects of being a youth minister is that the creative projects you get involved in enhance the joy of ministry as much as they engage and teach the children. From 1972-1974, Project Mexico organized three two-week trips from Kansas City, Missouri to the city of Cuernavaca and the rural villages of Ticuman and Alejandra.

Becky and Elaine were two of the many young people who helped raise the money necessary to pay for the forty-hour charter by Greyhound bus. The average cost per participant was the grand sum of sixty-six dollars. Father Jose Tlaseca, our host in Alejandra, arranged work programs, worship services, and plenty of time to enjoy the local hospitality. We also got a lesson about how hard it can be to affect change. Father Tlaseca had organized an agricultural cooperative for the benefit of the small farmers, and those whose interests were not served by the cooperative resisted it and branded him a Communist. Our first Sunday there, we arrived at the small chapel to find that all the pews had been covered in honey. We spent the day working alongside the parishioners trying to remove the protest material. The incident was a blessing in disguise because it strengthened the bond among us all. This was experiential church at its very best.

There were numerous takeaways from our "mini Peace Corps" visits, but perhaps none as significant as the understanding that we are all alike on this planet. Our final supper together was a special fiesta featuring a goat roasted on an open fire. This meal—a Eucharistic Supper of sorts where all were welcome—was a beautiful way to acknowledge and give thanks for our special time together.

Dear Pete,

Your eloquent appeal for pancake eaters was received with interest. Although I personally like pancakes, pancakes apparently do not like me. So, the best I can do is to enclose a donation to your Mexican project. I wish you the best of luck.

And so, my dear amigo, vaya con Dios!

Will Stanbury

My early exposure to the pristine sands of Cape Cod Bay opened my eyes to the wonder of the natural world. My adventures in India and Mexico during the early 1960s buttressed my belief that one can find both human and natural beauty in abundance anywhere on this planet. We started the St. Andrew's Mexico Project to let the kids experience for themselves the beauty of another culture and the interconnectivity of all humanity.

We raised the money for the trips by hosting yard sales, recycling paper and cans, and hosting the grand Mexican fiesta and famous pancake suppers. Another signature event was our attempt to break the Guinness World Record for reading the Bible. We staged the event in a heated trailer that we placed in front of the entrance to St. Andrew's. Over eighty different volunteers rotated in and out of our cozy, warm sanctuary to read the Bible out loud—from cover to cover—for one hundred straight hours. Hats off to those who read their one-hour portion during the "graveyard shifts" between 1 a.m. and 5 a.m. We even timed it so that we finished our Read-a-thon fifteen minutes before the Christmas Eve midnight service.[4]

Thanks, and *vaya con Dios*[5] to all who supported those great trips for the young people of Kansas City.

---

[4] We were disappointed to learn that there was no Guinness World Record for longest read, only the fastest read.

[5] This blessing—so often heard in Spanish-speaking countries—remains a powerfully simple blessing regardless of one's religiosity: "go with God."

Dear Sir: 8/22/74

Just finished the article on your taking the group to Mexico to help the poor there. As I started the article, my thought was [that it was] great for the Mexicans and great for the kids in [Kansas City to have] the experience. Then [I was] shocked and disgusted when I came to the part that I have cut out and enclosed. For a church and assistant pastor to do such an illegal act is terrible, and for the articles to be put in the children's luggage to make them a part of the deceit is disgusting. Training them that this type of conduct is acceptable is so disgusting that I am shocked that you wouldn't at least have tried to conceal it. Instead you have shouted it out to the press and for publication like it was something smart and you were the big smart man. For the church to do and condone such actions is terrible and I note that the leader, Father Kreitler, is being transferred to California, and glad his guidance of children in this area will be at an end. Hope the church will call his attention to this misconduct and try to stop.

Very truly yours,

[Unsigned]

Guilty as charged! I take full credit for "smuggling" vitamin pills and toothbrushes after we were advised that if we shipped them, they probably would not arrive at their intended destination. A volunteer parish dentist had secured the brushes from a well-known company and another trusted source had donated boxes of vitamins. The adult chaperones and I collectively wrestled with our decision. Ultimately, we decided that the greater good was that a small village in the middle of Mexico might learn about and adopt preventative health care through our visit and our contributions. So, we simply asked the kids to divide up the items and carry them in their suitcases. We travelled by bus for forty hours and the border guards did not even ask us to open the suitcases. I am sorry that my behavior offended this individual. Perhaps I was wrong in my decision, but watching children brush their teeth for the first time—and with such enthusiasm—seemed to make it all worthwhile.

I should also note that in the Episcopal priesthood, we are not reassigned or transferred. After five wonderful years and three memorable and transformative trips to Mexico with the youth group, I accepted a job offer in California, where I am proud to say I continued to work with young people of all ages. I have fond memories from over forty-five years ago of the youth at St. Andrew's Kansas City. Unbeknownst to them, their acceptance of and trust in me shaped my ministry. My appreciation is heartfelt.

Dear Mr. Kreitler,

On behalf of the Secretary of the Navy, Honorable John H. Chafee, I wish to thank you for agreeing to participate in the "rap session" on April 14, 1972.

Please come prepared to speak your mind. The Secretary is asking for your help in finding ways to improve the image of the Navy. He recognizes that you who are "youth oriented" know what young people think. He is coming here to learn from you.

Charles C. Richardson

Captain US Naval Reserve

I had completely forgotten this request from John Chaffee's office and I had to smile when I found it again. My father was in the Naval Air Corps during the Second World War and I was in Navy ROTC and a proud member of the drill team at Brown University. The Vietnam War coupled with my experiences in seminary changed my focus though, and I became a conscientious objector by 1972. I guess you can say I continued to serve my country as an advocate on behalf of our youth, whether they saw the military as an option or looked at alternative means of service, such as AmeriCorps and the Peace Corps.

I was impressed by the Navy reaching out to people like me who worked with the youth of America. Coincidentally, twenty years later our daughter Laura spoke at the National Press Club in Washington, DC as a representative of Eco-Schools in front of Vice President Al Gore and Senator John Chafee. I am not sure that I always know what young people think—I actually find that "mystery" to be part of the attraction of working with them—but Captain Richardson's letter does reaffirm the importance of a dedicated church youth ministry.

3/14/72

Dear Peter,

I felt your sermon on Bugville was extremely creative and meaningful, but Sunday's Sound and Light performance put it all together. For the first time in my life, I felt the desire to write a letter in response to a sermon.

Since you scarcely met me, you can't know that a little over a year ago I was told that I supposedly had terminal cancer. Being only twenty-seven years of age, this was not easy to accept. Fortunately, I am still here and winning my battle to live life. This past year I have obviously viewed my surroundings, my family, and my relationships as few people ever do. To me, your sermon carried a clear message to others of much that I have seen this last year: the fullness of life, the meaning of love, and the entwining of the Christian community throughout it all.

I hope others appreciate your message as much as I and, may I say, thank you for the experience.

Regards, J.H.S. Jr.

Every single person's story deserves a voice and an audience. This man's story made me cry. Being able to share in another's journey is part of a priest's privilege package. There are many components of that package and the gifts flow in both directions. We can learn valuable life lessons when someone takes time to share intimate feelings, viewpoints, and personal situations. Some people, like J.H.S. Jr., have a worldview that enables them to take life's curveballs and turn them into something positive. This young man's incredible attitude and infectious positivity resonated with me.

Role reversal is not uncommon in the priesthood; a parishioner becomes the teacher and we priests become the disciples or learners. I have others pastor me on a continual basis, as I have battled cancer a half dozen times and may have to undergo chemotherapy for the rest of my life. Years after J.H.S. Jr. wrote me, I was fortunate to meet author and professor Norman Cousins (1915-1990), who championed the effect of positive mental attitude on physical health. I invited him to speak at St. Matthew's, where he spoke about humor as an antidote for all aspects of pain or depression. As clergy, we have the opportunity to model behavior that signals that the glass is half full rather than half empty. Forty-six years later, reading this "twenty-something's" message emboldens this seventy-seven-year-old to keep up the good fight. What a privilege it is to possess such a letter.

Dear Peter,   *April 27, 1971*

I was glad to get your note about the success of your Walk for Mankind and that you had been able to go the whole route.

In my younger days, I was a good walker too. In about 1915 or 1916 I walked nine miles... in the Ozarks to a service on Presbyterian Hill, across the river from Branson, Missouri. Then, in 1921, I walked fourteen miles on a trip from Green Mountain Falls in Colorado, part way up Pike's Peak.

Now at eighty-one, I am not able to do that much walking, except in Spirit. During your walk I accompanied you and your young people in prayer and meditation and I feel that it is proper that I should pay for myself because I think I went all the way. So, I am sending you a check for ten dollars instead of the five dollars that I pledged.

Sincerely,

Lillian C. Ball

This is the type of note that makes all the hard work, late nights, and challenges of professional ministry worthwhile. I smile every time I read it. My elderly friend was born in 1890 and yet, in 1971 she was cool enough to support our twenty-mile parish fundraising walk. It was held on a Saturday and the next morning I could barely get down the aisle for worship because my feet were so swollen and sore. Twenty miles is a long walk, but her generosity touched me and we raised lots of money for the Walk for Mankind. Doubling her pledge reminded me of the poor woman at the Temple whom Jesus praised for giving two mites to the collection offering—a small sum, but a sacrificial gift of significance, indeed!

I participated in two other twenty-mile fundraising walks over the years, but I was relieved to discover that the Hunger Walk in Los Angeles was only ten kilometers, or a little more than six miles. I wouldn't have made it down the short aisle of St. Matthew's Church following a twenty-mile walk.

P.S. Ironically, this note was written on the one-year anniversary of my ordination to the priesthood on April 27, 1970.

2/2/18

Peter,

You may not remember, but you married us on Nov. 17, 1973 at Country Club Christian Church in Kansas City, Missouri. Bishop Vogel would not let us be married at St. Andrew's because Bud had a previous marriage. We have made it all forty-four years and wanted to share this with you!

Carol and Bud Price

To Carol and Bud's credit, and as a model for other couples, they recently renewed their wedding vows on December 1, 2017 at St. Andrew's Episcopal Church, Kansas City—the very church in which they could not be married forty-four years earlier. Thanks Carol and Bud, for sharing your wonderful story with all of us.

I have performed hundreds of marriages, and have stood alongside many who have seen their dream of a forever marriage shattered by divorce. What should be the position of the church at a time when people are hurting and trying to make sense of a difficult situation? Shouldn't the church enable well-meaning people to have a second chance? With guidance, counseling, and compassion, the church can offer "marital resurrection" to its constituents. Permission to marry divorced individuals means that many of my colleagues and I were able to marry again. If the church stands for anything, it is that new beginnings are always possible.

Carol and Bud, I look forward to celebrating your golden anniversary!

Even though I have been asked hundreds of times, it never gets old to hear, "Father Peter, will you perform our wedding?" Each wedding signals a new story and everyone's story is unique and special. Deborah and Larry Dunn sent me this lovely picture with the message, "It's about loving unconditionally, celebrating family and friends, giving thanks for our blessings all year long." This photo of the newlyweds posing happily, while their adult children from a previous marriage smile in approval, captures the "triumph of hope over experience"—the hope that comes with having a second chance. Frankly, "Second Chance" might be an appropriate nickname for Father Peter. I was given a second chance at the Loomis School; at the Lighthouse Inn on Cape Cod, where I was fired from my waiter position and rehired the next day; at Brown University, where I had flunked out but was readmitted following my sojourn in India in 1963; and after my divorce from my first wife in 1981, when Katy accepted my hand in marriage in 1985.

When the church stands in solidarity with those who find love again after divorce, we mirror the kind of community envisioned by persons of faith from many religions. My forty-nine years as a priest have offered me the opportunity to proffer forgiveness and acceptance to many—as countless have done for me over the course of my life. The gift of a second chance is extra special!

Father Peter's Thirteen Premarital Instructions

1. We remembered Peter's advice to make the bedroom special.
2. A sense of humor really helps.
3. I remember you said a partner not feeling "special" might be a contributor to unfaithfulness.
4. The comparison you drew between marriage and a railroad track and a seesaw.
5. Your explanation of the meaning of covenant.
6. Give gifts on special occasions; don't give garden rakes.
7. When you marry each other you also marry each other's family. Very true!
8. Just the fact that there was some premarital discussion was important.
9. Take the first step in a stalemate situation and be strong enough to overcome pride.
10. When we get into stupid arguments, it seems to help when we discuss our vows.
11. The analogy of the spoons—two people lying together in bed, in harmony—is critical.
12. The explanation of the opening two paragraphs of our marriage ceremony.
13. Most memorable instruction was to regard our marriage as setting an example to others.

Early on in my career, I sent a six-part questionnaire to approximately thirty couples whose weddings I had performed. I stated that I would not share the individual responses with anyone but that their collective answers would inform and help strengthen my premarital counseling. The list above is a compilation of what thirteen of those couples remembered most from my premarital instruction. Even if some of the recollections may not be *exactly* what I said, I believe engaging couples after their marriage in an exercise of reflection is a win-win undertaking. I learned a lot and I think the couples benefited as well from reflecting upon their experiences. You'll notice that I used the metaphors of a seesaw and the railroad track in reference to marriage. I told them that being up and down, like a seesaw, is normal in most marriages. I use the railroad image to paint the picture of both partners, as unique individuals, moving on separate but parallel tracks; if the marriage is tended to properly, the couple will appear—like the tracks in the distance—as if they are one.

Peter,

You creep—I just read your letter in The Messenger *and it made me cry. I really will miss having you here, but I'm <u>very</u> excited for you.*

    M.L.

I have only been called a creep once in my life, but M.L. was a gem, so I smiled when I first read her note from 1974. She was a parishioner who offered her artistic skills when we were refurbishing the Sunday school rooms. M.L. painted her super-graphic designs in colors that were welcoming for our eager students and that turned a concrete column into the tree of the knowledge of good and evil and a blackboard into Noah's ark, complete with giraffes and elephants gracing the bow. I learned early on in my career that every congregation is filled with capable people of all ages, many of whom simply need to be asked to release their particular talents. It is our job, as clergy, to encourage and embolden everyone in our congregations to share their gifts. We do not always know the full measure of the impact we are having on others until someone tells us so. Take the time to let others know how much they really mean to you and how much you appreciate their contributions. Not everyone can be a Picasso, but the varied gifts of a community of faith are the candles that brighten up the parish, just as M.L.'s paintbrush did.

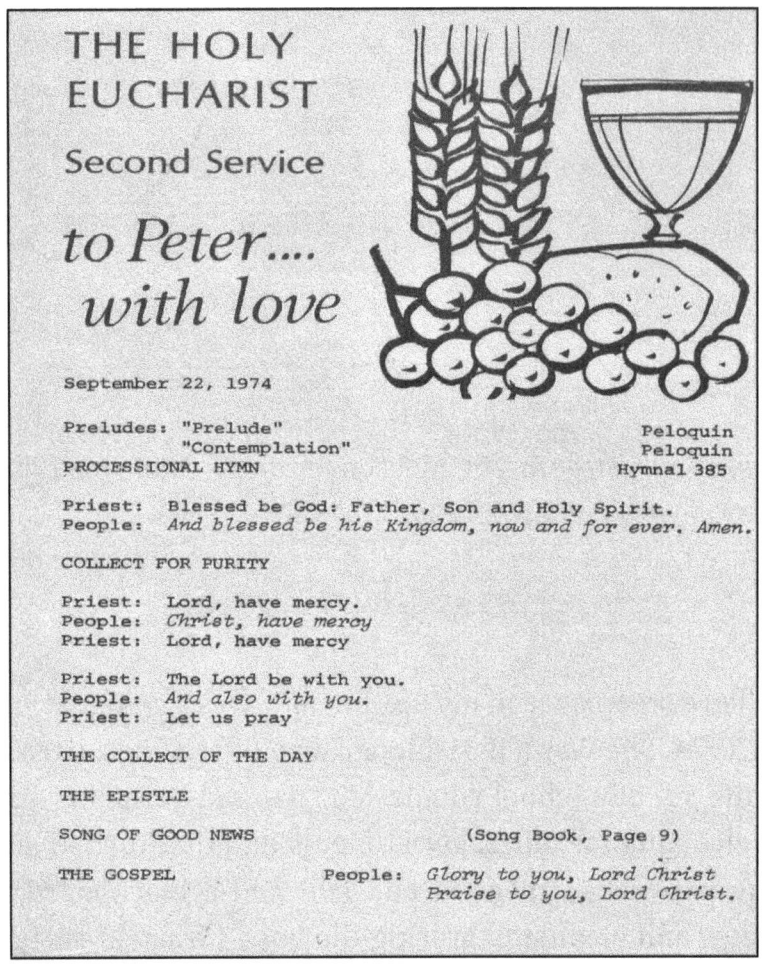

My career with the church began while I was in seminary, doing field work at St. John's, Lafayette Square[6] in Washington, DC. I began my full-time ministry in 1969 in the middle of America in Kansas City, Missouri. When I bade farewell to St. Andrew's Parish on September 22, 1974, the congregation said goodbye to me in a special way: *to Peter....with love*. I then ventured further west to Pacific Palisades, California. In 1990 I closed out my parish work at St. Matthew's and moved on to create Earth Service Inc., the non-profit environmental organization that I ran until 2016.

I am humbled by and grateful for the congregations of St. John's, St. Andrew's, and St. Matthew's and for those people with whom I have served in the environmental community. And so, allow me to return the words from this service bulletin and say, "to all with whom I have worked...with love!" Almost a half-century has gone by quickly and I wish my recall were total, for there are many people to thank along my journey. Suffice it to say that no individual walks the pathway of life alone. I am thankful for family, friends, colleagues, and the strangers who have reached out to me through the years. Your blessings to me have been generous and are appreciated beyond measure.

---

[6]St. John's Lafayette Square is located across the street from the White House.

Remember it is very important to have a tan the entire year. Don't smoke any dope, Peter. It could be the end of your young career. Be good, good luck to you...California Dreaming...Hmm.....

Allan Stark

Dear Peter,

Well, here I am in beautiful Windsor, Connecticut. Perhaps my destiny lies somewhere else. I never knew how much babysitting there was in a prep school. I do like the school and especially the kids though. Some of the teachers seem to be caught up in their own little worlds and big ideas. What a way to start off a letter! What the hell does a young minister, who has a great wife and two delightful children do in California? Certainly, he has a few drinks with the pillars of the community. He certainly has a few deep raps with a few confused, but well-meaning, teenagers. He probably does about the same things in California as he did in Kansas City. Except he may go to the beach with the kids. Remember it is very important to have a tan the entire year. Don't smoke any dope, Peter. It could be the end of your young career. Be good, good luck to you...California Dreaming...Hmm...

    Allan

Allan's warning ranks high on my list of the mentoring and advice letters I have received during my career. Oh, if we could all be so direct and honest. I laugh every time I reread "...have a tan the entire year. Don't smoke any dope, Peter. It could be the end of your young career."

Advice about appearance and behavior comes in many forms. My former baseball coach, Ralph Erikson, told our team one day, "I don't really care how well you play, but I do care how good you look when you play." My first boss, the Reverend Dr. John Harper, who was the rector of St. John's Lafayette Square, chastised us seminarians for crossing our legs during the service. Dr. Samuel Shoemaker Johnson, the rector of St. Andrew's who hired me for my first full-time job, advised me that the shoes I wore for Sunday services should be spit-shined to a high polish.

All the above advice may seem comical or nonsensical, but the point is well taken. Acting and dressing like a professional speaks volumes to parishioners. The words we speak from the pulpit are not the only things that people remember about us. Frankly, we are scrutinized for all of our lifestyle choices, even down to the footwear and clothes we wear. Many parishioners went out of their way to compliment me when I cut my long hair shorter. Listen to the practical advice that folks offer; it matters. And a special shout out for my young friend who wrote from my prep school alma mater, the Loomis School.[7]

---

[7] As of 1970, the Loomis Chaffee School.

Dear Peter,   *April 29, 1971*

Just for the record, I don't like form letters. I received [yours] today and I really think the remainder of the day will be a disaster. Can you imagine receiving a form letter on a cold, rainy April day? Let me answer that for you. On second thought, you know the answer. So, in the future, please question everything before you do it.

On a more serious note: if you can muster up enough interior strength, will you please write a letter to my draft board telling them that I am a very sincere young man. In other words, lie. Send it directly to my draft board. I am considering the possibility of quitting school. I can always return to college after I have served. I believe student deferments are wrong and unjust, but if you must know the truth, I am bored with school.

I would like to hear from you, but I will return any and all form letters. Peter, those were bad...Chris Smith got into Connecticut College and will probably be accepted at Vassar. God lives next door now, however, when the neighbors found out he was black they all moved. Jesus, his son, is not holding his age well at all. The Royals[8] are doing quite well. When they are down, step on them,

      Allan

I am unable to recall the form letter I wrote that caused his objection, but I get a real kick out of Allan's unique ability to express displeasure. I was especially impressed by this letter because, in my experience, folks are usually reluctant to be so direct with persons of the cloth. Perhaps because we present ourselves as inhabiting rarified air, people tend to use cautious language with us and avoid confrontation or offers of advice. Thankfully, the preponderance of correspondence that I have received over the years has been complimentary and sometimes even flattering. Letters from individuals like Allan seem to resonate on different levels though, and I appreciate them for their honesty.

I am sorry that I have not followed up with many of these letter writers during the past five decades, in part because I had buried these letters in my "shoebox." Now that I have rediscovered these letters, I can try and reconnect with their authors, as I did recently with Allan. Who knows? New beginnings can happen in relationships, even well into our elder years. Perhaps, like me, you might want to make time to reunite with the people from your past.

---

[8] Kansas City Royals baseball team.

November 5, 1978

Dear Father Peter,

Mrs. Van and I want to write to express our sympathy on the loss of your beautiful church. The only consolation is that it was God's will and He will see that you and your congregation soon have a new and even lovelier one. It was close to a miracle that your home was saved though—the fire came so near—and for your sake, and your family's we are thankful. The enclosed cassette cannot, of course, be a solace, but I hope it will be at least a diversion. It is titled THIS IS YOUR BANJO.

Again, sympathies and best regards,

    Sincerely,

    Louis Van Phalen

A few years before St. Matthew's burned to the ground, a family gave me three one-hundred-dollar bills in a sealed envelope to thank me for some counseling I had done. A year later, I read an advertisement in the newspaper about a tenor banjo for sale. My mother had played the banjo as a young girl, and I thought I would give it a try. One rainy day, I went to the home of an elderly gentleman—"C'mon over after my nap," he said—and he proudly unveiled a Paramount Style C tenor banjo. I gave him the envelope with the three hundred dollars inside—his exact asking price!

I certainly didn't expect Mr. Van Phalen to write to me a week after the fire, but I'm glad he did. His thoughtful letter and recording of him playing his 1927 banjo brought me comfort as I wrestled with losing our 1953 A-frame church. Mr. Van Phalen's kindness transformed a transaction—buying a second-hand banjo—into a connection. Thank you, kind sir.

Dear Peter,

I just wanted to tell you how much I've enjoyed your positive comments and conversations over the last few years. I'm going to miss having someone to laugh with as we pack bags at Hughes Market next year for the Thanksgiving Ingathering, too!

My very best to you always,

Jane

It took me awhile, but I slowly began to realize that modeling the words from the Bible often has a greater impact on others than preaching an eloquent sermon from the pulpit. "Getting my hands dirty" meant walking with parishioners on a hunger walk, packing bags for the needy during the holiday season, standing with teenagers in a court of law, picking up garbage from the beach on Earth Day, building homes for the homeless in Mexico, clearing brush to eliminate fire danger, or cooking Wednesday soup-night suppers during Lent.

The words from the classic melody, *Show Me*, remind me of Mother Theresa and Mahatma Gandhi, who manifested what I describe as the "theology of walking about." These heroes are two of the shining lights on a hill that have shown brightly throughout my career. I even made a pilgrimage, walking in the Punjabi summer sun for hours, to Gandhi's memorial site in India in 1963.

How we present ourselves in community speaks volumes about our priorities and lives. One of my professors at Virginia Theological Seminary, the Reverend Dr. Cliff Stanley, came into class one day with a torn piece of a grocery bag on which he had scribbled some notes. He explained, "I had this thought watching a young man help an elderly lady getting something off the shelf she could not reach, 'Good Samaritan?'" Thanks, Dr. Stanley, for taking the common and ordinary events in life and giving them everlasting meaning for our lives. And thanks, Jane, for refreshing my memory of finding joy in packing groceries for those who do not have enough to eat.

9/25/91

Peter,

I miss our Tuesday morning meetings and, for that matter, I miss you too. The very best of luck on your environmental odyssey. I am 100% with you on that.

    Peter Berrington

I never told the gentleman who wrote me this heartfelt letter of support just how influential he was in my life. I regret to this day that I never said thanks in a proper way. Peter's well-ingrained conservatism was rooted in his proper English upbringing, yet he was always willing to listen to the viewpoint of this Episcopal/Anglican clergyman and member of the Green Party. The way he challenged my position on issues openly, but always with respect and love, gave me hope for the future. I could not have asked for more of a friend thirty-five years my senior.

Peter lived into his nineties. He always inquired how I was doing and described perfectly my environmental focus as an "odyssey." I have always admired and engaged with my elders, from my grandfathers to parish and community members. I cherish the wisdom I have gained from them and will continue to maintain, enjoy, and benefit from these friendships. Never discount the accrued wisdom of those who live into their eighth or ninth decades.

Dear Peter, 5/11/92

I am writing to invite you to join the Environmental Leadership Forum of the California League of Conservation Voters. CLCV is the oldest and largest Political Action Committee for the environment in California.

Sincerely,

David Allgood

Southern California Regional Director

I have included this letter as an example of the wide range of gracious invitations we clergy receive. I have been asked to join the local Rotary, Optimist, and Lions Clubs, as well as to offer the opening prayer at the Riviera Golf Club banquet for the PGA golfers. Clergy are generally wired to want to please and to accommodate requests for their time. However, given the complexity of life today and the demands on all of us in the profession, it is wiser for us to discern ways to serve where we can be the most help. Saying "no thank you" every now and then is a prudent boundary that helps us to allocate our time better.

In this case though, I accepted David's invitation with pleasure. My involvement with the Environmental Leadership Forum was time well spent. I was able to break bread with Senators Barbara Boxer and Diane Feinstein and with Congressmen Henry Waxman and Adam Schiff, among others who voiced a commitment to preserving our fragile environment. I gained an appreciation for the demands of serving as a senator or member of Congress. I also began to understand that the fate of creation does lie, in part, in the hands of elected officials as well as appointees in the Department of the Interior and the Environmental Protection Agency. An important, and often overlooked, role that faith-based citizenry can take is to hold accountable those who are entrusted with the laws that conserve, preserve, and restore creation.

August 19, 1993

Dear Peter,

I am very pleased to hear about Environmental Clergy of America, and specifically about ECO America West. Thank you for also enclosing the Yellowstone Creed of Declaration.

I appreciate the invitation to serve as a member of the Council of Wisdom. You have anticipated my only reservation. I am having to turn down all invitations that involve commitment to more meetings. Since you do not expect that of me, I will be glad to help in any way I can.

Sincerely yours,

John

John B. Cobb Jr.

Doctor John, professor emeritus of theology at Claremont College, author, eco-theologian and "wisdom keeper," is one of the most respected and articulate persons I have ever had the pleasure of meeting. His 1970 book, *Is It Too Late? A Theology of Ecology,* caught my attention because it addressed, sooner than most, the looming environmental crisis. I then read his paradigm-shifting *For the Common Good,* written with Herman Daly of the World Bank. What an eye opener!

The last time I saw John in person was when he presented a lecture to the Orange County Interfaith Coalition for the Environment. He was ninety years of age, sharp as a tack, and—with passion and specificity—still ringing the alarm bell about creation's collapse. My admiration and appreciation for this humble person of God will endure forever and I would encourage anyone to read both of the books I referenced above. In particular, his explanation of the importance of the Greek word *oikos*[9] should be required reading for all clerics and laity alike. As this modern-day prophet used to tell me, "**to see the world with ecological relations at its core means never to see it the same way again.**"

---

[9]The balance and interdependence of ecology and economics, i.e. the management of the biological and the business sides of the household.

Dear Mr. Kreitler,

In June 1992 a historic Earth Summit is to be held on the environment in Rio de Janeiro. Persons from all over the world will meet to debate what can be done to stop the unmaking of creation on the planet. Hopefully, this body will draft some new agreements that can take us a step toward a better future for our children and ourselves.

Sincerely,

Owen D. Owens

Director, Ecology and Racial Justice

National Ministries, Baptist Church

In retrospect, this was perhaps one of the most significant letters that I received during my career. I had left parish ministry to serve as the first minister to the environment for the Diocese of Los Angeles a year before this defining gathering in 1992, and Owen's note was the first time that I had heard about the upcoming Conference on the Environment. I chose to go and obtained a press pass from the United Nations so that I could function as a photographer and observer of the official proceedings and the events hosted by the non-governmental environmental organizations that attended. During my two weeks in Brazil, I attended talks and marches, explored the Amazon Basin, and enjoyed the generous hospitality and "upper-crust" lifestyle of my former fraternity brother, Don Pearson. Don had made his home in Brazil and thanks to him, I was able to experience the country through the eyes of a local as well as through the lens of my camera.

I had embarked on my sabbatical in 1990 in order to discern the future of my ministry. Two years later, the Earth Summit validated the direction my priesthood was taking and reinforced my commitment to lend my voice, vision, passion, and knowledge to the preservation of the incredible creation we have inherited. I learned a great life lesson: be open to the still, small voice within calling you to explore new paths in service to God's creation. It dawned on me in Rio just how daunting the call from scripture to "till and keep the garden"[10] would forever prove to be. What can Peter do to stop the unmaking of creation? is my daily personal challenge. Thank you, Owen, for presenting me with this opportunity.

---

[10] "The Lord God took the human and put him in the Garden of Eden to till it and keep it" (Genesis 2:15). All quotations from the Bible are taken from The New Revised Standard Version.

Peter,   *4/29/92*

You have honored my family in a way that has never been done in the past. You have recognized that which motivates me, that which drives me, that which guides me—the holy meaning of the work that I do in preserving that which our God has created for us. Peter, I was truly moved by your presentation and spoken words. Your photographs are a vision of peace and creation. Certainly, while it appears that you are the person that types the words and snaps the shutter...we both know that your hands are guided by God.

    Love,

        Bill Taormina

This gentleman owns and operates a large trash hauling and recycling business. His compliments about my presentation and my ability to use a camera to document the beauty of creation were capped off by his words "we both know that your hands are guided by God."

I find "picture sermons" to be an especially powerful messaging medium. In one that I called *Joy in God's Creation*, I compiled three hundred and fifty images that I presented using five slide projectors, three screens, and two dissolve units. I also had exhibits of my photographs of trash that I collected from the beaches of Cape Cod and Santa Monica Bay. The shows were titled *Extinction* and *No Es Basura*, which translates from Spanish to *This Is Not Trash*. The purpose was to make people aware that discarding trash, especially plastics, into our oceans is hastening the death of a resource that gives life to all.

As creation rapidly slips through our fingers, we must heed the warnings of scientists, especially our climate scientists, and focus on sustaining the greatest gift ever given: our fragile island home.[11] Whether you lend your voice via the written word or visual image or whether you simply lead by example, all of us can do our part as stewards of creation to impart the message that every action we take and every decision we make has an environmental consequence.

---

[11] The Book of Common Prayer, Eucharistic Prayer C, page 370 refers to our planet as "this fragile earth, our island home."

Dear Dad,

I know this is late, but happy (belated) birthday. I just wanted to let you know that I wish we had spent more time together this summer, but just so long as I know you haven't forgotten about me...Thanks for everything and I wish I could have given this to you on your real day!

    I love you!

    Jen

Daughter Jennifer is a letter writer like her stepsister Laura. She used to write from college and still continues to send cards and letters.

Jen, supportive wife of Mark and mom of Theo and Megan, placed her career as a marriage and family counselor on hold to raise the children. My relationship with Jen, however, has been affected by the dilemma facing those of us in service professions: the struggle to balance parenting and home life with the demands of ministry, in whatever form that ministry may take. She has confronted me about my tendency to focus on others more than her, and I have to admit that at times I have been guilty of that charge. Caught up in the demands of being a parish priest, I once spent seventeen straight evenings away from home attending meetings. Not good, indeed. Tears come to my eyes when I recognize that hundreds of people have remarked that just having me be there for them was enough to make a difference, but Jen, perhaps more than anyone else, has felt that I have not always been there for her. No excuses can undo the past, but as brother Brad has often remarked, "Things will get brighter."

You were great! Your introduction was the best I have ever had. Dinner at my place...soon![12]

    Ed Begley Jr.

Introducing someone whom I respect and admire has been one of the four greatest privileges of my priesthood. The other three are performing a baptism, officiating at a wedding, and being asked to offer a eulogy of a person whom I knew well and admired.

Ed Begley Jr.—actor, activist and decades-long visionary spokesperson for the environmental movement—accepted my invitation to speak at Virginia Theological Seminary (VTS) and I was asked to introduce his main talk. Ed received a much-deserved standing ovation from the hundreds of clergy and seminarians who attended his talk. The event spoke volumes about The Episcopal Church and about Ed personally. Being inclusive, willing to take a risk, and open to new ideas and ideologies are three key attributes of VTS and of The Episcopal Church in general. I once heard the Anglican Primate of Canada speak to the General Convention of The Episcopal Church about the interplay of the secular and the religious when it comes to preserving the creation entrusted to us. In Ed Begley Jr. we have a role model for this nexus of the secular and the spiritual.

Engaging, knowledgeable, low-key, and inspiring are just a few of the words that begin to capture this icon. Most important, Ed walks the talk. Mimic the behavior of this modern-day prophet and the world will thank you.

---

[12]Ed sent his message via text; this is the only digital communication I have included in *Dear Father Peter*.

Sunday Oct. 26, 1980

Dear Fr. Peter,

You once said you looked to the altar guild[13] ladies as your surrogate mothers, and now, as one of those mothers, I hurt very deeply and sincerely for you. If caring helps, I certainly do.

Dorothy Lindstrom

Here are two firm facts to which all members of the clergy would attest enthusiastically:

    1. We rely on lay people to help us do our daily job.

    2. We are fortunate when a person in our own congregations assumes the role of pastor for us in our times of need.

We are all—regardless of title, wealth, status, or power—vulnerable at times. Clergy of all faiths are human beings first, family persons second, and clergy third. We experience the joys and sorrows of life just like everyone else, and we never forget it when someone writes a heartfelt note of empathy like Dorothy did.

Dorothy was a loving, caring, and nurturing individual who perceived my real hurt even though I had not said a word to her about it. This role reversal and mutual support are two more reasons why communities of faith are such important institutions, especially in our increasingly impersonal and "I-centered" culture.

---

[13] Members of the altar guild help clergy do their jobs by setting up the church for services every single week of the year.

Dear Peter,

I am aching to tell my sadness to someone. Yesterday [brought] the shock and sadness of the space shuttle, and today I found out I have lost a friend.

Carol was the counselor I liked so much. I read she has died. Last August when she said she could no longer see me because of her health, I was bitterly disappointed. She said I had so many goodbyes she hated to add another, but it wasn't really goodbye [and] we would keep in touch as friends, and I feel such a loss. I guess I was depending on her to be there.

Now I'm crying again.

Patsy

My late friend Patsy was a voluntary breather—she had to take each breath consciously and had to sleep in an old-fashioned iron lung. If she were to fall asleep out of her chamber, she would have died. We were close in age, yet the restrictions that she had to endure were daily and demanding. She simply could not function alone. Despite her hardships she found a way to find joy. Her brother Barry and others built a series of tables to hold her plants that allowed her to prune her garden from her wheelchair. I would bring communion to her modest home on a regular basis and we would sit in her backyard amidst her bonsai and succulent plant collection that she nourished and tended.

I have never encountered anyone who was as constantly challenged and yet as optimistic as Patsy. Her spirit and her positive attitude amazed everyone who took the time to be with her, so it was doubly hard to see her in pain over the loss of her dear friend Carol. I was sad when Patsy died, but I carry the gift of her spirit and her acceptance of her lot in life with me to this day.

March 15, 1989

Dear Reverend Kreitler,

Thank you very much for your genuine concern and support regarding my matter. Your letter was very helpful and beneficial with regard to resolving my situation. The outcome decided by the court revolves around me being on probation for three years and participating in a work furlough program for thirty days.

I am dedicated to making sure that I never find myself in another situation like this again. I can honestly say that this has been an experience that I will not forget and it has taught me a great deal about drinking and driving and the tragic consequences that result from this. Thanks again.

Very truly yours,

[Name Withheld]

I was profoundly sad to learn of this young friend's premature death. I was very familiar with his struggles and rereading this letter so many years later makes me tear up at the indiscriminate nature of addiction. It spares no one. In a culture that promotes social use of alcohol and some drugs, young and old alike are awash in compromising situations that often end in sadness and grief.

The prevalence of drugs and alcohol in communities of faith requires a clergy person's continual attention. Opioids get much of the attention today, but heroin, cocaine, cigarettes, beer, liquor, and marijuana also destroy families and individuals in dramatic numbers. We must, as caring communities, acknowledge this systemic cultural scourge without pointing the finger of righteous indignation.

February 11, 1991

My dear Peter,

You told me of your decision to leave St. Matthew's and the slide show in my heart began. It covers a lot of years, but even so much more. [The] services, retreats, parties, picnics, meetings, weddings, funerals and the jeep ride to the amphitheater, and, and, and, and, and... then my own family album—you've seen us through it all...[helping] my mom move along and move out, counseling most of us at one time or another. You've always been there for us and we've all loved you for it. Now you're moving along and I think your decision is a good one and I hope you'll let me go with you. I don't want to stop adding pictures in my album. I'll miss you smiling at me from the altar each week but I'll look forward to all those others times yet to come.

Much love always!!

Carol

If there was any family throughout my career who exemplified the calling as being a part of the priesthood of all believers, it was Carol's family. Carol's dad was an Episcopal clergyman and her mother, Kathleen Morse, and Carol's Aunt Connie were two great examples of why we should never relegate the elderly "to the pastures." Upon reflection, these women were probably the first two senior citizens, after my grandparents, who had a big impact on my life.

We who are in the public arena must on occasion step back and thank the men, women, young people, and children who trust the clergy enough to come and hear us share our views, our theology, and our personal stories. The people make the church, and we leaders can only shepherd their good works. For me, Carol represents the many wonderful individuals who love their God and God's creation.

P.S. Happy ninetieth birthday to Carol!

Don't let the lobsters and steamers throw you off stride. We want a slim, trim preacher in the fall.

    Senator John Tunney

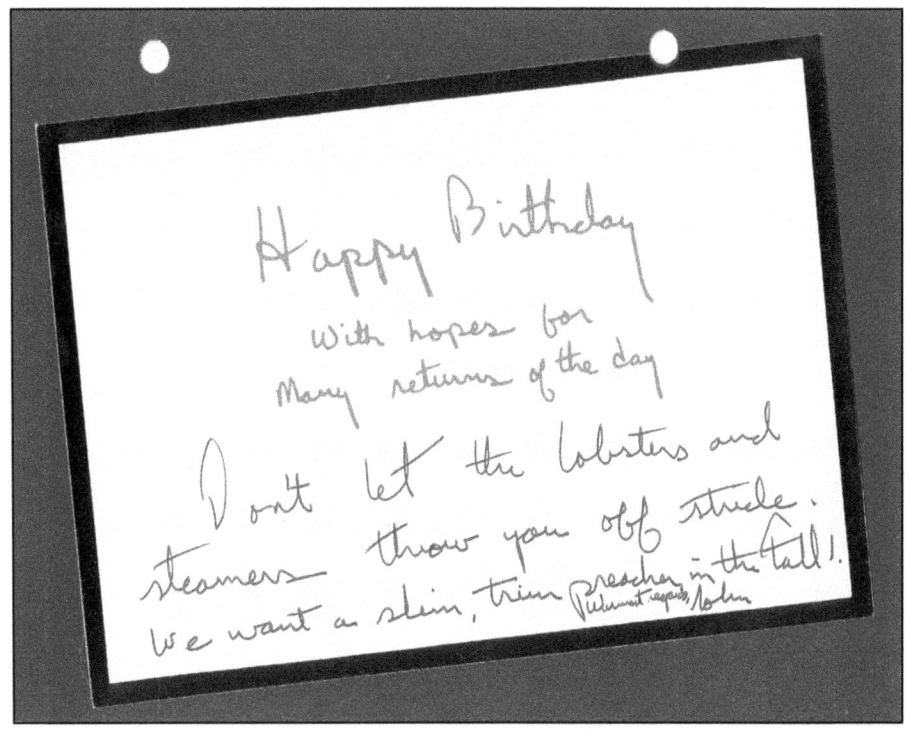

The late Senator John Tunney of California was one of my favorite friends and he and I broke bread together frequently. John, the son of boxing heavyweight champion Gene Tunney, was conversant on many subjects, an expert skier and tennis player, and a great family man. He, his wife Kathinka, and their daughter Tara were members of our parish school community. John encouraged me to become more politically savvy since politicians and their decisions influence issues, such as immigration and the stewardship of the environment, that resonate with our Judeo-Christian heritage. How right he was!

After twenty years of parish ministry, I was weighing whether to embark upon a career in politics or in environmental preservation and education. As part of my discernment process, I set up thirty-five breakfast and lunch appointments with people whose advice I valued. John was one of three politicians, along with Congressman Mel Levine and City Councilman Marvin Braude, whom I interviewed. I launched each discussion by asking my dining partner what gave him or her meaning in life. Their most common refrain boiled down to "being in the natural world with the people I love." The other take-away that stayed with me was John and Mel's warning against a political career because the travel between Washington, DC and California is demanding and takes its toll on family life. These tableside consultations gave me a lot to think about and were instrumental in helping me to chart the next steps along my path and in my decision to answer the call to engage in environmental ministry.

> **CHEVY CHASE**
>
> *In my experience there is nothing harder to fold than the American Flag, with the possible exception of a contoured sheet. God bless America.*
>
> *Chevy Chase*

"Stargazing" is a daily part of life for those of us living and working in the environs of Hollywood. Katy and I got to know Jayni and Chevy Chase when their three girls attended the parish school at St. Matthew's.

Celebrities live in a world of mixed blessings. I have developed great respect for those in the public spotlight, especially those people who are chased by the paparazzi. Living in Los Angeles we get to see it all, and fame is not always fun. Public figures, like all of us, appreciate privacy. Most clerics do not have celebrities in their congregations, but we all must be mindful of the larger lesson—so well ingrained in seminary—that the church welcomes all. We do not get to choose who comes to us. All are welcome at the table.

Clergy are public figures as well, and our lives are often scrutinized, dissected, and discussed—sometimes negatively. Our spouses and children may be considered fair game also. Learning how to handle living under the microscope can make or break a career.

One day Chevy and I were talking about a long-term project that I was working on about the American flag and patriotism. He offered to write something for the book jacket and sent this wry note to me.

Dear Peter,

Last Sunday as we were standing in the church, christening Piper, I felt for the first time as if I were not standing in a place [where] I didn't belong. Perhaps it was because of your experiences, shared with me that day, that provided a space for challenge and questioning in a house I had always seen as pious and righteous. Perhaps in seeing some of its shortfalls I was able to see its tremendous potential. But if I am true to myself, perhaps I was in need of a place. Perhaps, confronted with the shortfalls of my own house, my own family, my own self, the idea of unconditional love seemed appropriate and necessary. As we read from the prayer book, as I watched you place the water on the forehead of my child, and as we lit candles, I felt a decided comfort take hold in me through the practicing of ritual. There was a strength I found in the baseness of it, the imperative of it, and its endurance.

There have been many times in my life when I can and have said that I have had a spiritual experience. Most often these have come at a time when I have endured long periods of isolation. In this sense, they have been highly personal, emotional, and possibly intellectual. There have been other times when I have seemed to visit a spiritual place, in Mexico, Santa Fe, or Peru. Never have I experienced the spiritual in the presence of my family, in the church of my family, or acting with my family.

There came to me for the first time Saturday a feeling that I did in fact have my own family. That I had created something wholly other than my first family, my parent's family. I wanted this feeling to endure, to carry with me. To place in perspective all the other workings in my life. I seemed to find the possibility of that in the ritual... As I have come to know this past few years, the important thing in life is not control, but the ability to lose it. The capacity and strength to go where your instincts, your creativity, even your faith will take you. I can see in ritual a strength and solidity that through practice would not confine, but would provide the means to let go.

There is something magical about watching the water pour from your hand onto Piper's forehead. Something I did not see with Hailey. Perhaps it was because of all the other children that were there. Perhaps it was because I had a family there that was my own. Perhaps it was because I was ready to see it. My family [is] blessed to have you as a friend. There is a continuity you have brought to our lives that no one else could.   Tucker

This well-written, thoughtful letter from a long-time family friend captures the privilege, joy, and special nature of being a priest. Thank you, my friend, for being who you are—a talented teller of stories, a lover of family, and a gifted, thoughtful teacher for me and others. I'm honored to be able to share your letter with a wider audience because in it you eloquently express a keystone element of the spiritual journey.

April 23, 1981

Dear "Wise Counselor,"

Just caught your articles in Redbook*. Congratulations on getting the job done and I look forward to the whole book. Clergy bear an even heavier load in this than most in that we are vulnerable as is every other person, but we are the representative "good ones" in the community...and somehow not supposed to be vulnerable—Tough!*

Best,

Bob

I was blessed to begin my full-time career working with three exemplary members of the clergy: Samuel "Tobe" Shoemaker Johnson, Stan Ramsey, and Bob Schenkel. All three were mentors to the neophyte Kreitler serving at St. Andrew's, Kansas City, Missouri in 1969. Bob's astute commentary about the dilemma faced by people helpers in general, and clergy specifically, is one reason I wrote the book *Affair Prevention*.

Echoing Pittman McGehee's famous comment that "clergy have the availability of vulnerability," Rev. Robert D. Schenkel Jr. points out that our collar does not make us immune to the human temptations. Adultery, affairs—or whatever euphemism is used to describe extramarital sexual relations—affect thousands of lives every year, including those trusted with offering help to others. As one wiser than I advised me years ago, it is the strong person who can ask for help. Indeed, if you're in the helping world and in danger, ask for help!

Dear Pete,

I wanted to write you as the days are winding down to next Sunday, ending your regular involvement, with your last sermon at St. Matthew's.

Mother and I want you to know how proud and excited we are for you in the new ministry you are undertaking. We have a pretty good idea of what you are putting together and, as parents, remind you of the need for diligence, caution, and patience in this venture, recognizing that there could be difficult days ahead. In the past, you have, in our eyes, been eminently successful and, given adequate time, you would expect the same in the future. You have certainly brought much happiness to us, for which we are most grateful, and we will pray for a successful and satisfactory new beginning for you. Good luck to you and God bless.

> *Love,*
>
> *Mom and Dad*

Even as mature priests, it is of greatest significance to be affirmed by our parents because we are always their children. I chose not to follow in the family footsteps of pursuing a career in business and it means a great deal to me that my parents accepted the choices that I made. Mom and Dad did not always agree with me and scratched their heads at some of my decisions, yet they encouraged me to fly on my own as a young man. They were always there to pick me up when I fell, and to the end of their lives, they offered advice and words of encouragement, which I took to heart. In this letter of support, they reminded me of the "need for diligence, caution, and patience." Oh, how right they were.

In essence, *Dear Father Peter* is a testimony to my parents and grandparents on both sides, in part because they were prolific and thoughtful letter writers. To hear their words of praise sounds different than those expressed by any other people in my life.

Dear Peter,

Thank you so much for coming to the preschool chapel this morning and sharing your musical talents, wit, and wisdom. I know all the teachers enjoy continuing this Christmas tradition.

I am always very touched and grateful when busy people like you are willing to give their time and themselves, to enhance the life of the children.

Sincerely,

Eileen

Eileen Doyle

Director Early Childhood Education

St. Matthew's Parish School, Pacific Palisades, CA

I've enjoyed working with children since my days as a sailing counselor at Camp Monomoy. I spent the first five years of my priesthood as the youth minister at St. Andrew's Church in Kansas City. I enjoyed creating meaningful and fun activities with the teens such as publishing a newspaper, decorating a "hang-out" in the basement, and traveling to Mexico to work in poor villages. During my seventeen years at St. Matthew's, I spent every Monday morning with three-to-five-year-old children. I think I was the only priest in the diocese at the time who had chapel for that age group on such a regular basis. I loved it. To this day, almost forty-five years after I started The Preschool Band, I am invited back every year to play—not very well—my 1927 four-string tenor banjo along with the talented parents and faculty. I am not an accomplished musician but, after all these years of trying, I can handle the repertoire of "Silent Night," "Jingle Bells," and the all-time favorite, "Rudolf the Red-Nosed Reindeer."

The youngsters' spontaneity and honesty taught me a great deal about human nature. One child described God as an old man sitting on a throne in heaven being fed grapes by angels. Close enough! Every clergy person should be required to spend at least a couple of years teaching the very young or, rather, being taught by the youngest among us.

When you are front and center on a weekly basis as a pastor, priest, or rabbi, it's easy to wonder if anyone is listening. A common and recurring nightmare among clergy is that our carefully crafted words will fall on deaf ears.

This fourteen-word note reassured me that my message was indeed resonating with the kids in the congregation. I was especially grateful to receive this compliment in light of the frustration expressed by one of my then-teenaged children, "Dad you are so good with everyone else's children; why are you not so good with us?" There is nothing like the bluntness of your loved ones to keep you humble, but when a young person takes the time to write, find an envelope, affix a stamp, and send a letter, it takes the sting out of the more brutal feedback we receive.

Sarah's note—complete with original artwork—is a great example that a letter's word count is not as important as the sincerity of those words. We should always remember the powerful impact that simple expressions of appreciation and encouragement can provide.

SOFTSEL COMPUTER PRODUCTS

February 28, 1989

The Reverend Peter Kreitler

Dear Peter,

Because you and I have been such good friends, I decided to put you on the cover of our magazine. I was lucky enough to find a picture of you in your twenties, when you were a war correspondent taking photographs during World War I.

Warmest personal regards,

Mike

Michael D. Pickett

President and Chief Executive Officer

Leading social scientists like Dr. Norman Cousins have encouraged the use of humor to mitigate the stress associated with challenging personal and professional times. I subscribe to this theory wholeheartedly and—as my parents intoned and studies have shown—I also recognize that humor is an asset in strong relationships. Mike was the best man in Katy's and my wedding in 1985. We were born decades after World War I, but I got a kick out of Mike's shot at our advancing age. He was born one day after me on July 22, although he is *many* years my senior. It's a shame he did not send a copy of the picture that reminded him of me.

Too often, humor is underrated and underused in ministry because it can be tricky to determine appropriate situations and audiences for our levity. Tears and times of sadness are a natural part of a long ministry and, at times, laughter can be a healthy, mitigating asset. And if laughter is the best medicine for our own tough situations—and to keep us from getting too big for our own britches—then I have a lot of dispensing pharmacists for friends. Their humor, playful sarcasm, and hyperbole keep me humble. Besides, Mike—as usual—was incorrect; I was a World War *II* journalist with a Kodak Brownie camera.

May 15, 1995

Dear Peter,

Your presence in Sacramento was successful beyond expectations and was an initial step toward fulfilling my dream of an activist clergy protecting the environment.

Let's talk when possible about where we go from here. A first step might be to send a wider mailing to clergy...asking that they formalize a network of clergy for creation.

Best personal regards,

*   Tom*

California Senator Tom Hayden

Chair, Natural Resources and Wildlife Committee

California Senator Tom Hayden and I became friends. This well-read, competent intellectual and I loved to talk religion, politics, and baseball. Tom dreamed of bringing people of all disciplines, especially clergy, to the table to find ways to conserve, preserve, and restore Mother Earth. He recognized that all of us are dependent upon healthy ecosystems—clean water, soil, and air—to sustain life. He viewed the imperative to honor these resources as a directive emanating from scripture. He challenged me to preach and teach the environmental ethic wherever I went.

Tom was a passionate advocate for the earth who was ahead of his time. Even in death, his voice has not been muted because he spoke truth about the fate of our planet. Sometimes even secular humanists have a deep and abiding spirituality and a love of creation and his prophetic words ring true today, more than ever. Voices raised in concern over the degradation of creation emanate from many walks of life. Our responsibility is to listen and then act!

Dear Peter,

Thank you again for preaching. We've been blessed.

Prayers for you and creation continue.

In His grip,

Bob

Trinity Episcopal Church

Peer appreciation is the highest form of praise a preacher can receive. For a member of your own "team" to say thanks is a gift that is precious in its rarity and simplicity. The words that form a sermon are rarely chosen randomly or without a great deal of thought. At the end of each service, preachers wait for meaningful feedback or an acknowledgement of the effort they invested in the sermon. It is a special occasion when a colleague gives two thumbs up to your sermon. Preaching is a privilege and, hopefully, practice eventually makes perfect. As an instructor at the College of Preachers once counseled

1. Tell them what you are going to tell them.
2. Give them your message.
3. Tell them what you just told them.

This is a good rule of thumb for crafting those precious minutes that many people consider to be the highlight of the worship service. Another best practice for clergy persons who are confident in their own preaching is to invite guest preachers who have subject matter expertise that is of interest to their congregations. Collegiality strengthens the whole of the church.

I THOUGHT I'D DROP YOU A LION

Dear Father Peter,

Thank you for your very nice note and query. As you know, I had a severe heart attack last year; this holiday season I had a petite mal. All in all, in less than two years I've been hospitalized three times. Recently I concluded thirty daily x-ray therapy treatments (radium) for cancer at St. John's as an outpatient. The prognosis is good, but you can understand my health has been a problem and a horrible expense and trial.

I hope to become more active in church, however, in truth I must tell you that sometime ago I became greatly disillusioned in my church—the secular sermons, the new prayer book, and the church's great involvement in the National and World Council[s] of Churches, for [which] I have no respect.

Dear Father Peter, *would you please do me a great favor of considering this letter confidential? I thank you kindly.*

Cordially Yours,

[Name Withheld]

This letter captures the challenges facing many aging Americans today. The elderly can feel especially afraid of the unknown. At the same time that their bodies are failing them, their churches and neighborhoods are changing, and friends and loved ones are dying. It all makes for overwhelming, disorienting, and scary times. The church doors must always remain open to those who feel lost.

I could feel my correspondent's heartfelt agony over not finding solace and comfort in the church she loved, but I was encouraged that she could reach out to me through this letter. I have withheld the writer's identity in deference to her request for confidentiality. Instead, I hold her name near my heart as one of the great ladies who felt comfortable enough to be honest and forthright with me, even though I was almost fifty years her junior. This letter is the only instance during my career that I have received a dual salutation. "Dear Father Peter" is special enough, but to have that repeated in the same note reaffirms the warm sentiment—in fact, it gave me the idea for the title of this book. Besides, you've got to love her humorous pun: "I thought I'd drop you a *lion*."

The Episcopal Church of the Good Shepherd Search Committee

May 31, 1991

Dear Father Kreitler,

You have been suggested to the search committee of Good Shepherd, Dallas, Texas as a person to be considered as a candidate for our next rector.

We would like to know if you are interested in being considered for this position, fully realizing that you will want to see that and the profile for a rector before you can begin serious consideration. If you would like to be included in our search, we need to know that your church deployment profile is up to date or that you will update it for this search.

Please let us hear from you.

B. C. (Robby) Robertson

Chairman

Most priests, rabbis, imams, or ministers view being the leader of a community of faith as the ultimate achievement. I was no different—until I began to preach about the collapsing of God's creation. My first inkling that I might be called to environmental ministry was when I reflected on a talk that I gave to the Barstow School on November 6, 1970. Twenty years later, I was flattered to receive letters of inquiry about becoming a rector of an Episcopal parish, but I politely declined all those invitations. I loved parish work, but around the time of the first Earth Day,[14] I felt drawn to lend my energy and voice to the chorus of concern over our fragile island home. My mentor John Seely guided me through a rigorous process of reflection to identify how I might serve the highest good. This invitation from The Episcopal Church of the Good Shepherd arrived at the same time that I was launching my environmental ministry. I believe we can serve our fellow human beings and God in a variety of roles. In my new ministry, the earth would be my parish.

---

[14] April 22, 1970.

Dear Peter,   *June 1, 1998*

Thank you for including me as one of your guests on Kaleidoscope. *During my career as an environmental advocate and sometimes government official, I have been interviewed many times for many different types of news and public affairs programs, but I have never been asked such thoughtful questions or had the opportunity to talk about my views and values so candidly. It was quite a liberating experience. I believe that the format—an opportunity to get acquainted in a relaxed and friendly way with a card-carrying environmental activist—is quite inviting. The intellectual content is much higher than usual because of your advance work in formulating the questions, but the discussion stays grounded in practical, even earthy, details that keep the discussion relevant. The old adage for the environmental movement, "Think globally, act locally," takes on new meaning as we approach the millennium, with disappearing species, vanishing supplies of water, and buildup of greenhouse gases at the top of the list of threats to human dominion over the planet.* Kaleidoscope *offers a unique model of citizen engagement at the local level in developing fresh ways to sustain life and advancing new visions of sustainability. The program deserves to find a wide audience.*

Yours truly,

Mary [D. Nichols]

Mary's thoughtful and affirming commentary about our TV show validated our work and emboldened me to continue for another twelve years of production. We closed shop in 2010 when mantle cell lymphatic cancer took its toll on my energy levels. Since then, I have continued to follow the careers of many of the environmentalists I interviewed, including Episcopalian Mary Nichols, who was appointed chair of the important California Air Resources Board by former governor Arnold Schwarzenegger. Affectionately called the "Queen of Green" for her proactive leadership on climate change, Mary has, in my estimation, exemplified what it means to be a person of faith in these challenging times. There is no other theological issue as important as sustaining a healthy planet. Mary's service to both country and creation represents the best in public service. Over lunch one day, Mary prophetically advised me, "Peter, if you are going to deal with the biological issues of the planet, you will, of necessity, have to address economic issues as well." Her leadership has been honored in many sectors, and I add my admiration for her persistence—a key ingredient for success in any endeavor, especially environmental work.

You are launched!

Fear not—the water, the air, the fire, the earth will support you.

Sister Miriam Therese MacGillis, Genesis Farm

Dear Peter,   *3/25/91*

You are launched!

Fear not—the water, the air, the fire, the earth will support you.

I love that you are an earth <u>servant</u>—once that is put out with clarity it will draw energy to itself—you will be led where to go.

Keep in touch,

Blessings,

    Miriam

    Genesis Farm

When I found myself at a crossroads wondering whether to go into politics or environmental work, I was fortunate to be able to take a three-month break from parish work to begin my discernment process. I spent my first week in New York with Father Thomas Berry, who wrote the seminal book *Dream of the Earth*, and in New Jersey with Sister Miriam Therese MacGillis of the Dominican Order of the Sisters of Caldwell. I was blessed indeed to be in the presence of these two Roman Catholic "saints" as I began the sabbatical that reshaped my entire ministry.

Sister Miriam founded Genesis Farm in 1980. Genesis is a sustainable farm and center for teaching about spirituality and the environment. She taught the value of a dollar by example. I can remember harvesting dandelions for our evening salads and ferreting out treasures from trash at yard sales. Her leadership as an environmental educator and mentor emboldened me to continue in her footsteps. When I began the nonprofit Earth Service, she wrote, "You are launched!" Her letter is equal parts celebration, appreciation, and reassurance and is sealed with her blessings. Her blessings touched me and today I often conclude my letters with the same heartfelt valediction.

Father Peter,

Came by for our counseling session at 12:00 pm. Hope we had not made a mistake about the time. Will call you on Monday to reschedule.

Happy New Year,

Mimi and Eric

Mea culpa, mea culpa—my fault, my fault! Though I do not recall the situation described, I accept the blame. Remembering personal appointments and being on time or at least calling if delayed—we're all tied to that cell phone on our hip after all—are essential practices in a successful career, especially in the helping professions. Mimi and Eric left me one of the most important reminders that I have ever received of the value of showing up when you say you will. It was just a note left at my office door, but it addresses a key ingredient in developing trust between a clergy person and her or his parishioners.

Recently, Katy and I attended a wedding where the priest, dressed in his street clothes, was arranging the candles on the altar at the time the nuptials were supposed to begin. The officiant was the only one who was not on time and he kept the guests wondering and waiting until the service finally started—twenty minutes behind schedule. Yes, there are rare instances in which unusual traffic or emergencies disrupt our plans, but being late or not showing up at all is, at best, inappropriate.

Dear Father Kreitler,

I'm impressed by the galleys you sent me of your forthcoming book, Affair Prevention. *This is a remarkably moderate and pragmatic examination of both the realities and the ethics of the sexual relationship. It throws a refreshing light on a preoccupying problem of our time.*

I wish you well with it, and hereby give my permission to quote from this letter to assist in its promotion.

    Cordially,

        Charlton Heston

The ethics of the sexual relationship is a key indicator of the health of a marriage, and in the fall of 1969, I had a real wake-up call about the role that this topic might play in my pastoral counseling. A parishioner called on me and wanted to know how to handle his girlfriend. Apparently, she was jealous that he had set up his mistress with an apartment and a car. Oh, and by the way, he was married with two children. Wow, above my pay grade right out of the starting gate! This incident made me realize that the issue of adultery was destined to come up often in my career. As a result, I decided to invest the time and effort to become more fluent in the threats to fidelity and the countermeasures one can take to protect the marriage covenant. I did research, conducted interviews, and ultimately wrote a book on marriage and adultery. I knew about Charlton Heston's love of reading, his strong marriage, and the weight that his opinion carried, so I sent a draft of the book to him.

My premonition and Charlton's response were prescient. I have spent countless hours with many couples addressing the havoc that cheating has wreaked on their relationships. *Affair Prevention* and Mr. Heston's commentary were written thirty years ago, but—in part because we are constantly bombarded by television and newspaper stories glorifying extramarital affairs—adultery continues to degrade the health of marriages. Infidelity truly remains "a preoccupying problem of our time."

To whom it may concern,

Please mail me information regarding your class "Affair Rejection."

    Thank you very much.

        Linda Loren

In the fall of 1979, I advertised that I was going to teach a class at St. Matthew's on marriage and extramarital affairs called "Affair Prevention." About twenty people signed up. Perhaps I should have called it "Affair *Rejection*," as was noted in Linda's letter. Friends of mine joked that if I wanted the class and the companion book to sell out that I should call them "Affair *Promotion*."

In my premarital counseling I always discuss these four pillars of a strong relationship:

1. Good communication
2. Conflict resolution
3. Intimacy skills
4. Knowing each other's life script or family story

Discussing intimacy skills leads to the topics of sex and sexuality, which in turn introduces the subject of marital fidelity. The sexual relationship is often the barometer of how a marriage is succeeding. Roughly fifty percent of marriages are in danger of being compromised by adultery. The Ten Commandments got that one right. As Linda states, affair rejection is prudent advice.

Pastor Peter,

I was very surprised to find the enclosed article in the Daily Bruin[15] *and, having found something in it potentially embarrassing, thought it wise to bring it to your attention. In the first quote given you state that you've lost "many good friends and relationships to affairs." The ambiguity of this statement could lead one to believe that through your own philandering you have lost many good friends.*

Now, I, as a former employee of St. Matthew's, and one who truly saw the "dirt," can testify to the absolute spotlessness of your character. I hope my raising this point will be some aid in the construction of future press releases and that, this grievous matter excluded, everything goes well for you.

    Sincerely,

        Lance Jorgeson

A cleric is often the subject of cocktail party conversation, especially in small communities where everyone knows everyone else's business. You can double the gossip factor when your name appears in magazines, newspapers, or college bulletins. Quadruple the attention when the subject matter is controversial, such as extramarital affairs. In those instances, one can almost expect barbs and misinterpretation, yet Lance tried to help me out. The single biggest criticism levelled at me during my career is that I have openly addressed matters perceived to be political or otherwise inappropriate for a pastor's commentary. Topics that have provoked consternation include adultery, war, gun control, justice and equality, and the environment. Thankfully, because I have always tried to be a pastor first, my parishioners often cared about me, protected me, and got past our theological and political differences.

I value The Episcopal Church's tradition of bringing reason into an understanding of the Bible and history. History and literary criticism have been indispensable tools in my attempts to address tough topics creatively and effectively. An effective ministry depends upon the wise counsel of others. Thanks, Lance, for having my back.

P.S. Those five issues listed above still need our undivided attention today!

---

[15] *The Daily Bruin* is the Brown University newspaper.

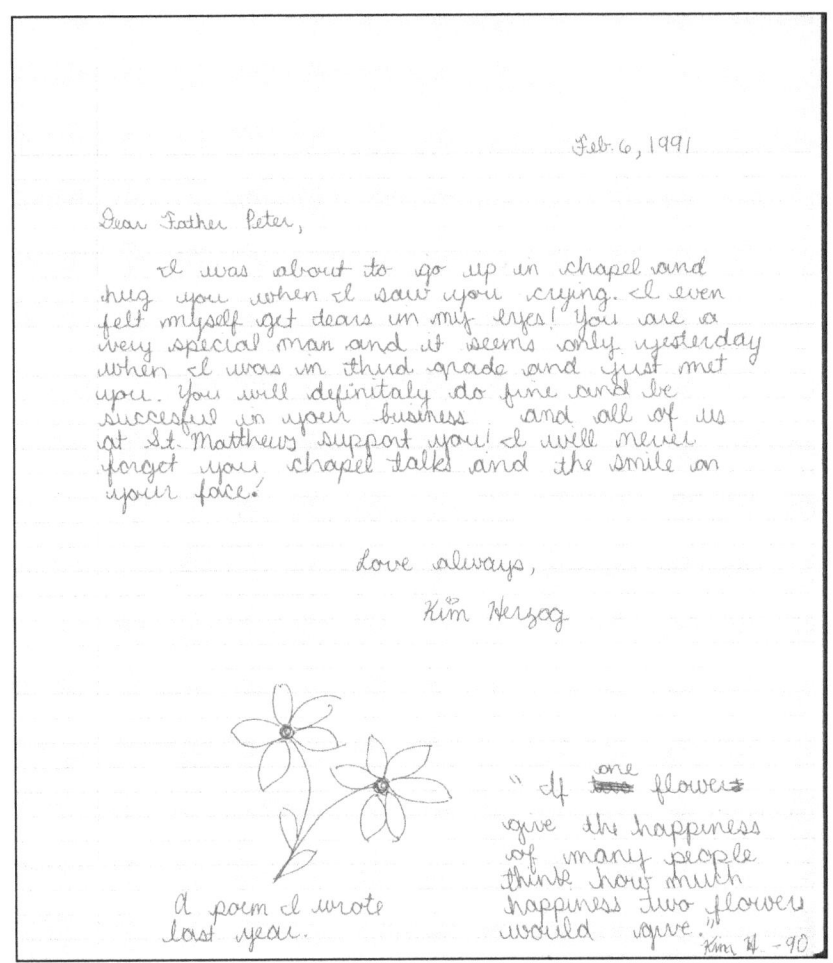

Kim's empathy was on display from an early age; she wrote me this touching note of concern when I was preparing to leave St. Matthew's Parish and School and she was in the sixth grade. Rereading her letter thirty years later, my first thought was that it was not surprising that she had become a rabbi. Kim serves the congregation of Temple Emanu-El in Dallas, Texas—the largest Reform Jewish congregation in the south—and has been a leading advocate for immigrant rights. I am sure she is a "flower" radiating happiness whenever she touches the life of another. She certainly put an eternal smile on my face with this remarkable note.

As I compile this collection of letters, I am reminded of the advice of a mentor of mine, Mr. Frank Davis, former chief counsel for MGM Studios, who said that how you say goodbye is of greater importance than how you say hello. Kim certainly gave me a great send off!

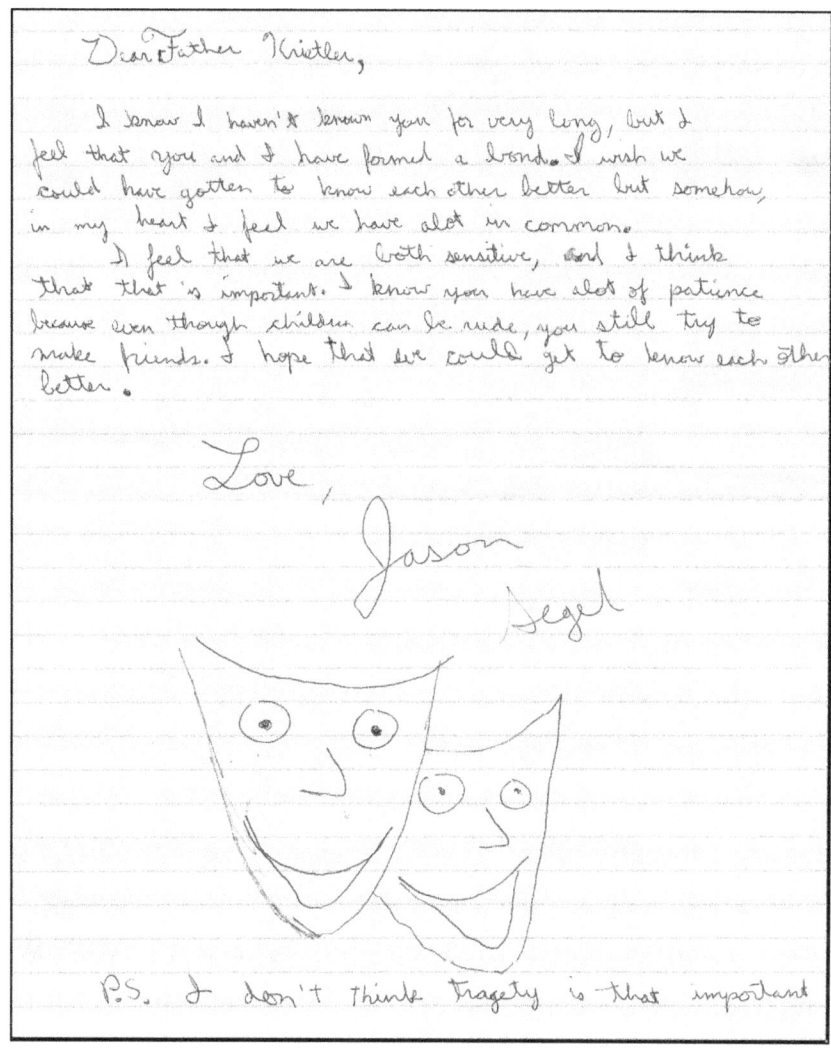

I am proud to say that Jason was another of our daughter Laura's classmates. His successful acting, directing, and producing career is something I have watched from afar and, once again, his note reminds me that the pupil often becomes the teacher.

Jason wrote this note when he was in sixth grade. I am flattered that he felt a particular kind of bond with me and that he recognized at an early age that sensitivity and patience are key factors in developing strong relationships with young people. It's not surprising that Jason, who admitted early on that he did not think that "tragety" was that important, has made his mark by bringing humor to the screen. I agree; when you can find humor, especially with young people, you can build bonds more effectively and easily. Keep up the good work, Jason!

Dear Peter,

Thanks, good brother, for the good words of encouragement and support. Thanks too for your prayers on April 1. We and the homeless can certainly use all the prayers and help we can get.

Either the President will give us the building or we will take up residence in Lafayette Park.[16] That, of course, means that we would almost certainly be arrested. It was just last week that the Supreme Court heard arguments in <u>Clarke v. CCNV</u> and committed themselves [sic] once again to the proposition that sleeping is not a constitutionally protected activity for the homeless as a means of political expression and seeking official acknowledgment and help. It's God's choice, of course.

A telegram from y'all to the White House asking on behalf of the homeless certainly couldn't hurt, if you find yourself with the time.

God Bless,

Mitch

In 1984 I had the good fortune of spending a four-day weekend at The Community for Creative Non-Violence (CCNV). I had read in the news that its founder, Mitch Snyder, an outspoken advocate for the homeless, ran a center that fed its clients with food gleaned from grocery stores throughout Washington, DC. Mitch would also go on extended fasts to bring attention to the plight of those who had no place to lay their head at night. I asked if I could visit, observe, and learn. While there, I participated in peeling away the wilted leaves of discarded lettuce to reveal a healthy core. I ate as a strict vegetarian for the first time in my life, had nightly discussions with Mitch, and I realized that "sainthood" isn't limited to old bearded men from the distant past.

Mitch and the staff of CCNV lived out the gospel of caring for the least among us. I came away refreshed and hope-filled that Mitch's voice and actions could raise public awareness of the plight of the many displaced persons struggling right here, in the richest nation in the world. Six years later I mourned his tragic death. He was a voice for the homeless that has not yet been duplicated. He lived the words: "come unto me all you that are weary and are carrying heavy burdens, and I will give you rest."[17]

---

[16]Coincidentally, the park is across the street from St. John's where I did my seminary fieldwork.
[17]Matthew 11:28.

Dear Peter,

You looked handsome at Holy Eucharist. Your good thoughts and kindness always show in your eyes and face.

You surely have assisted in bringing faith and healing into the lives of our family and friends.

How fortunate is our Diocese of Los Angeles for you to become Minister to the Environment!

    Jacque and Dick

This elderly couple faced many hardships with an attitude that some might even call saintly. They became models of grace for me and I still try to mirror their example.

In our tradition we emphasize the idea of the priesthood of all believers. Ordained or not, The Episcopal Church affirms that we are all called to exercise the qualities of kindness, compassion, understanding, forgiveness, and love towards our fellow human beings. Too often, we overlook the humble among us who quietly serve their God and their church without reward or acknowledgement. One does not have to wear a collar to have a meaningful impact on the lives of others.

How fortunate are we, as clergy, to have parishioners who care enough to offer such a caring send off.

January 20, 1992

Dear Peter,

What can I tell you...I cannot believe she's gone. I can't believe she'll not see Max and Dana grow up. I can't believe that I will never see her again. It hurts so much at times...and yet at other times, I'm OK, really fine. I don't understand much of all this. But I know that she's not here anymore and I miss her very much. "Till death do you part" are really words, because death doesn't help very much. I feel apart physically, but emotionally it's far more complicated...you are a good friend, you are a part of my life, Peter.

    With love,

        Sam

I had the privilege of marrying Melanie and Sam. To then grieve with this friend who had lost his wife at an early age made me realize that we priests do not have all the answers. The Episcopal Church and other communities of faith have their own time-tested rituals that can help us to process what is hard to understand. Yet when you sanctify a marriage one year, then rejoice in the birth and baptism of children, only to have your life upended when cancer claims someone so vibrant, it is understandable to push back against God and ask why. Why did God take one who was so beautiful, kind, loving, and young?

We clergy receive many letters expressing profound sadness and confusion. Words may be inadequate to the task of helping another feel whole again, but the presence of and a caring hug from a representative of God can be very comforting and restorative. The bereaved never forget our prompt and thoughtful responses, just as we never forget receiving such notes. Never!

My only regret is that the challenges of aging can make it difficult to stay in touch with the many people who have crossed my path during my half-century in the priesthood. Maybe social media—with its instant gratification and connection—does have a purpose after all.

Peter,

I have talked with this girl, fifteen years old, who has been doing dope (pills, acid, speed) for five or six months. She realized she was pregnant around Halloween. So, her parents have found drugs in her possession. So, they lock her in her room after school. Last Thursday she looked real doped on acid or something. So, she went to Boulder, Colorado to see her sister (with parents' permission) and while she was there, she had a very insufficient abortion. She told me that there was a radio going, some friend of her sister's came in and gave a fix of morphine or heroin. She said she was scared out of her mind and it hurt like hell. And she told me she had to talk to someone. I just called Ecstatic Umbrella and some cat named Paul said for me to talk to my friend tomorrow and tell her a few of the dangers, like blood poisoning, internal bleeding, and she also has a need for speed and acid or just plain pills, so it's plain to see she needs a shrink. For her and her parents. Paul suggested Doctor………a shrink at KU Medical because he is not uptight about drugs, just wants to help people getting screwed up on them. My mom says she might have dreamed this up—being pregnant—but I doubt it. What am I gonna suggest to her tomorrow…she may hate me but I don't want her to die of something. Help me, please. Thanks,

John Doe

Receiving a letter like this in the beginning of one's career is very sobering. John Doe presented himself as a good friend trying to be of help. Before I responded, I asked myself, Have I had the training to deal with the challenges this letter presents? Am I out of my league entirely? Should I call and recommend a specialist? Throughout my priesthood, I have received many requests for help covering a wide spectrum of subjects, and each time I ask myself these same questions. In this case, I felt the circumstances warranted that I seek additional resources and support. Perhaps I am naïve, but **I think a good pastor should also recognize her or his own limitations**. I preface all pastoral counseling with the caveat that if I can't be of help, I will let you know and will try to find someone who is better able to respond to your situation. As such, in both Kansas City and Los Angeles, where I have exercised my priesthood, I have developed relationships with a group of counselors, psychologists, and psychiatrists.[18] I have relied on these professionals for advice and have referred people to them when necessary. This letter made me cry when I received it and still does to this day. No child should have to experience what this fifteen-year-old endured, and especially not alone.

---

[18] I am especially grateful for the five years of years of psychoanalytical training I had with psychiatrist Dr. John O'Hearne of Kansas City.

I am wheelchair bound and on a ventilator. While I am, with God's help, working on my recovery—something no one has ever done—I am also preparing for the opposite. While I always enjoy seeing you, in this case I am requesting a pastoral visit to discuss, among other things, memorial service arrangements.

Steven Bridge

Dear Peter,

It's been a long while since I've seen you and in the interim, I have contracted Lou Gehrig's disease. All I can say is, if you have a choice, skip it. I am wheelchair bound and on a ventilator. While I am, with God's help, working on my recovery—something no one has ever done—I am also preparing for the opposite. While I always enjoy seeing you, in this case I am requesting a pastoral visit to discuss, among other things, memorial service arrangements.

There is no wild urgency, so come at your convenience. I live at the Sea Colony now. I look forward to seeing you.

Best Regards,

Steven

Steven's memorial service was held on a bright, sunny day at a cemetery in Santa Barbara, California overlooking the majestic Pacific Ocean.

The adjective *majestic* also applies to Steven and his remarkable approach to a disease more debilitating than any I have ever known. He kept his sense of humor, even as life ebbed from him in a more intense way each hour. Steven's story is a powerful reminder for us, who are still on our journey, to take each day one at a time and as a gift.

New York Yankee and Hall of Fame baseball legend Lou Gehrig died of Amyotrophic Lateral Sclerosis (ALS) in 1941. Today, in honor of his stoicism and grace in the face of this pernicious disease, we commonly refer to ALS as Lou Gehrig's disease. While he didn't enjoy the same celebrity as Gehrig, Steven was just as inspiring a role model for me. I am so delighted to catch a glimpse of Steven every time I see his daughter, Whitney, for she possesses the same spirit as her dad.

Lou Gehrig and Steven. Oh my, what examples these two men are for those of us facing challenging illnesses today.

10-10-84

Dear Father Peter,

Greetings! Just wanted to let you know that being married is a real kick in the pants. I love it. It's fickle—some things that never mattered before are now very important and other things that use to worry me are gone completely.

I'm writing this letter because you said you would not marry strangers, so you're stuck with my occasional greetings. You don't have to write back—I know you're busy as a beaver. If you ever move, however, let me know so I can bug you wherever you go!

I hope you are well and in shorts, t-shirt, and "tennies."

>*Love,*
>
>*Julienne*

One of the great privileges of being a priest is that you are authorized to perform weddings. In an Episcopal wedding service, we require that the couple confirm in front of family and friends that they are entering into marriage lawfully:

> *I require and charge you both, here in the presence of God, that if either of you know any reason why you may not be united in marriage lawfully, and in accordance with God's Word, you do now confess it.*[19]

Thankfully, I have never once had to disrupt the solemn occasion with a trip off-camera to discuss the issue raised.

Julienne's remark that I never marry strangers stems from my practice of initiating dialogue with every couple I marry during a minimum of five hours of counseling. I also offer a warranty card requesting a follow-up visit six months to one year after the marriage.

P.S. I loved Julienne's mental image of me in my casual attire in Southern California.

---

[19] The Book of Common Prayer, p. 424.

The Elmwood Institute

Dear Reverend Kreitler,

Thank you very much for your kind letter, which reached my office while I was on a lecture tour in Europe. Your sermon moved me deeply, and I hope that you permit us to reprint part or all of it in the Elmwood newsletter. I shall pass it on to our editor, and will ask her to get in touch with you directly.

Thank you for your generous support of the Elmwood Institute and for your offer to lend us your "fairly strong voice." I'm not sure what would be the best way of making use of your offer, but publishing your sermon and making it available to our members may be a good beginning.

With my very best wishes,

Fritjof Capra

I regret that I never had the pleasure of meeting this octogenarian thinker, physicist, writer, and founder of The Center for Ecoliteracy in Berkeley, California. If I had had the pleasure, I would have expressed my appreciation for his concept of the Web of Life, which has been pivotal in both the sacerdotal and environmental aspects of my career. The concept that we all are relatives and that every thread in the fabric of life is interwoven makes it easy to love all in creation.

Mr. Capra also helped me to understand that the words we speak from the pulpit may, by the grace of God, be given a wider audience than we ever envisioned. If we cast our collective wisdom to the wind, as Mr. Capra has done for decades, who knows where the seeds may take hold?

Dear person who really is full of nonsense speaking on KABC radio...

I couldn't believe a person can have the nerve to call himself a [reverend], let alone claim to be of any church with such teaching. Is it any wonder our society is what it is—if you preach or teach such nonsense? If you preach and teach this—that is what we will have. Let's hear the <u>Word of God!</u>

I shall pray for you! Man, you really need it. I want a firm foundation to stand on, not quick sand. Get with it!

  Ten families from Van Nuys, CA

Once again, I include another "wake up, Peter" letter, this time from an anonymous group of ten families. Several of my Sunday sermons spawned similar criticisms. Even within my congregation, there were parishioners who characterized my preaching about water, endangered species, climate change, and global warming as "just another one of Peter's 'save the whales' sermons." I could handle the metaphor; the real disconnect was with those people who did not equate a sermon about stewardship of God's creation with preaching the Word of God.

This unsigned letter—though I did know it came from a nearby town—asked that I provide "a firm foundation to stand on, not quick sand." Ironically, this letter strengthened my messaging because it prompted me to frame my discussion of the environmental movement in theological language. I often refer to God's creation slipping through our fingers like sand. In addition, I reiterated via the media of television, radio, and newspapers that our first directive from our Judeo-Christian heritage was to keep and serve creation. The word of God in Genesis 2:15 is clear: sustain the foundation of the healthy ecosystems that you have inherited, and keep them healthy forever!

P.S. Thank you, "ten families," for the prayers and if any of you are reading this, give me a call. I would love to speak with you today—over thirty years later.

Thursday

Peter,

I would like to talk with you. I know what a hassle and a discouraging experience trying to visit this jail could be though, so I've put your name on my visitor's list. It would probably be the only chance for a session I will have for a while.

They're planning to make a decision about me very quickly, an estimated five days from today.

Hope to see you, if not in the immediate future, perhaps under more comfortable circumstances later. Thanks for your letter.

[Name Withheld]

Occasionally the phone call comes in the middle of the night, or a letter arrives from a friend in trouble, or word is passed from another about their family member who has cancer. These are the "drop everything" scenarios—the times when a person's whole world is turned upside down. The letter I shared earlier from Steven wanting to talk about funeral arrangements, or the anonymous letter about the young friend on drugs, or this one from a parishioner in jail—these situations demand immediate attention.

I have been the first call following a spouse's death by suicide, when a small child drowned in a hot tub, and when my bishop, the Right Reverend Robert Rusack, suffered a massive heart attack. I have sat on several beds with family members as we joined hands with the deceased and said prayers. Words can be hard to come by and often feel inadequate, yet they are never really as important as being there. While I never ever liked visiting jail, especially with young people who were caught possessing drugs, I showed up because that is the best response for the situation.

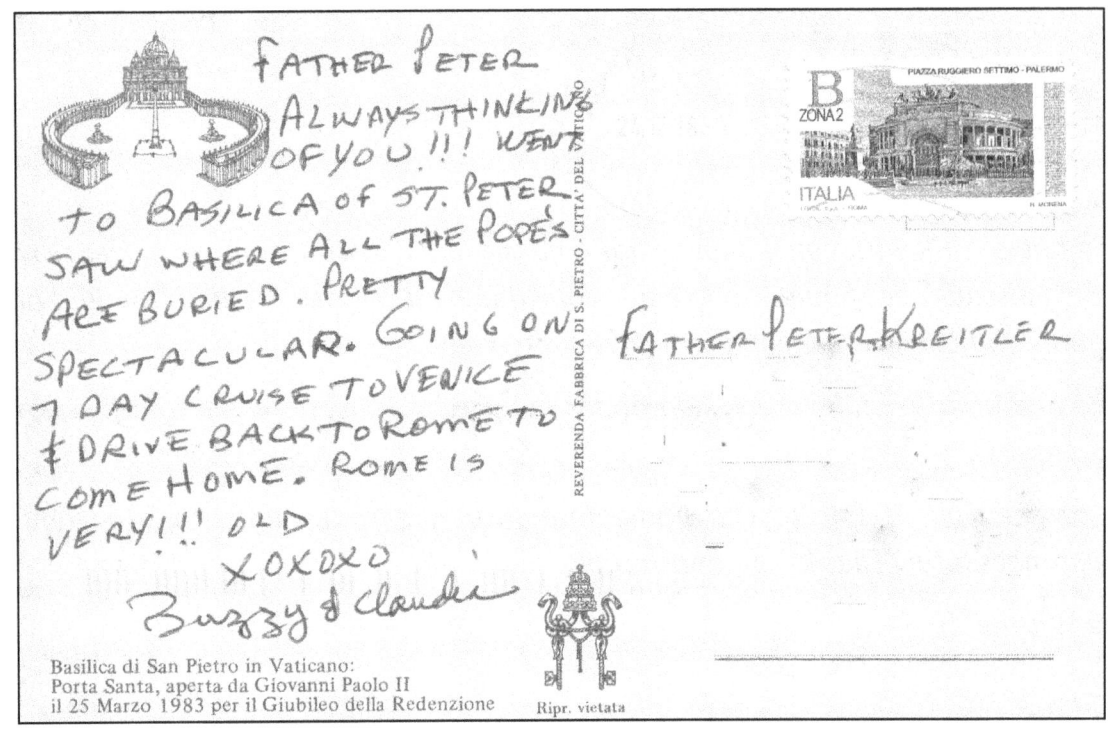

Buzzy is the only peer who always refers to me as Father Peter regardless of context or situation. He and Claudia sent me this postcard from Rome in January of 2019 and it immediately brought a smile to my face. Once again, there was his customary and favorite greeting: Father Peter.

My mother told me that she named me Peter because it meant "rock." Only later did I learn that Peter was also one of the first disciples called by Jesus.[20] Peter was a fisherman—a noble, challenging, and rewarding profession and a life-long favorite hobby of mine.

This postcard's smile factor was magnified because Buzzy was at St. Peter's Basilica, thought of me, and took the time to write. Even a simple postcard can reinforce the bonds of friendship. Wonderful! Thanks, Claudia and Buzzy.

---

[20] "And I tell you, you are Peter, and on this rock I will build my church…" (Matthew 16:18).

Dear Fr. Kreitler *4/10/85*

What a treat it was to have you join us yesterday at the Needlework Guild meeting. I not only enjoyed listening to you speak, but felt that I had actually learned a point or two that I plan to use in my marriage. I think that most of the women left with a good feeling that they had had an enjoyable meeting, yet there was food for thought. On behalf of the Needlework Guild, I would like to thank you for speaking to us. I am sure our paths will cross again.

Sincerely,

Nanci A. Twerdahl, VP

Whether to accept or decline an invitation to speak is an individual choice, but I have always found it difficult to decline most engagements due to the sincerity of the offer. Clergy are often asked to address a variety of subjects at churches, schools, or service organizations. I have spoken to groups that run the gamut—from the Daughters of the American Revolution and the National Society of the Colonial Dames of America to the Orange County Interfaith Coalition for the Environment and the Chamber of Commerce in Kansas City, Missouri—but I think that the Needlework Guild tops my list of unusual speaking venues.

It bears repeating that balancing the demands on our presence and time is a life-long challenge for members of the clergy. However, I have always viewed invitations to speak as a privilege and as an opportunity for learning as well as teaching. Indeed, leaving the "comfortable pew" of my own congregation was a wonderful way for me to grow personally and professionally. Make sure to allow time for questions; understanding what is on the mind of your audience can help you to introduce other dimensions of your topic.

Executive Office of The President

Council on Environmental Quality

Washington, DC   20503

April 2, 1998

Dear Peter,

I truly enjoyed appearing on Kaleidoscope.[21] I commend you on your efforts to raise public awareness of critical environmental issues through your show. It is through efforts such as yours that we are able to make a difference in the protection of our environment.

Again, thank you!

Sincerely,

Katie

Kathleen A. McGinty

Chairman

P.S. All the very best!

When I began my environmental work through Earth Service, I established the *Environmental Roundtable*, which hosted eighty-five different guests over its six-year run. Many folks encouraged me to turn these breakfast gatherings into a TV show, which I did in 1997. When I was a boy, I was taught to strive to do my best, so when I started booking my television show I tried to find the best speakers from across the country. Calling the White House was a bit daunting, but Katie was lovely and agreed to appear on the show. Under President Clinton and Ms. McGinty, the Council on Environmental Quality was proactive and effectively supported an environmental agenda. We eventually produced and aired 265 different shows over a twelve-year period. As one of our first guests, Katie set the bar high, but I was impressed by the quality of all the individuals on the forefront of this critical, all-consuming, global issue. Environmentalists are often criticized and maligned, but history will show that many are modern-day prophets who are no less important to our culture today than were Amos, Jeremiah, and Isaiah to their communities in the Middle East.

---

[21] Later renamed *Earth Talk Today*.

Dear Mr. Kreitler,   *5/16/91*

Thank you for contacting me about the Northern Rockies Ecosystem Protection Act. As you may know, this legislation would set aside sixteen and a half million acres of wilderness in Wyoming, Montana, Idaho, Oregon, and Washington. In addition, the bill would classify several rivers as "wild and scenic," provide protection for "biological connecting corridors" to aid wildlife migrations in the region, and direct the Department of Interior to conduct a study of possible national park units at Hells Canyon in Oregon and Idaho, as well as along the North Fork of the Flathead River in Montana. This legislation was introduced in the House of Representatives; however, comparable legislation has not been introduced in the Senate. I appreciate receiving your views, and rest assured that I will keep them in mind should the legislation come before the full Senate.

Sincerely,

Diane Feinstein, United States Senator

I have been criticized for writing a book about marriage and infidelity, preaching about the environment, and "wasting my time" writing letters to politicians about issues that people feel are unrelated to serving God. I have also been praised for all of the above. When people ask my wife Katy what her priest husband does, she responds, "He tries to preserve things." And she's spot on. I have preached and taught about the sanctity of the family, the value of the Bible and other scriptures in making sound decisions that will have long-term consequences, and about the importance of actively conserving and preserving the totality of creation entrusted to us. Preserving the national parks and wilderness assures our children and grandchildren will have a healthy environment to enjoy. I have created programs for youth, the community, environmental education, and a host of other initiatives as my way of serving my God.

One of the first letters I wrote as executive director of Earth Service was to Senator Feinstein, whom I had met through the California League of Conservation Voters. I had visited the beautiful national parks of California and—since the book of nature has always been one of my teachers—I wrote to encourage her to keep the Northern Rockies Ecosystem Protection Act at the top of her priorities. Planting seeds in the hearts and minds of others has always been a priority of mine, whether from the pulpit, through my writing, or by direct actions. When speaking to secular audiences, I would use the language of scientists, biologists, and educators in addition to theological jargon. Thank you, Senator Feinstein, for using your voice to help protect creation for generations to come.

Avenue Pictures

Dear Peter,

Wonderstrands is thoughtful and heartfelt in communicating the fundamental importance of environmental concern. Your depiction of the people and the piece is rich and convincing. Would I make this movie? Unfortunately, the answer is no. My reasons are several.

With very best wishes, Cary

Columbia Pictures Television

Dear Peter,

You must remember that I have written many scripts that either did not sell or were sold and should not have been. I've made so many mistakes that I've finally become something of a student of them. Wonderstrands has many interesting elements, but there are several structural story problems.

Best Wishes, Hugh

P.S. I never get my stuff right 'til about the fourth draft, if ever.

When you pursue a highly public profession like the clergy, public office, or a career in the entertainment business, be ready for rejection. One of the hardest aspects of life is being passed over or even just hearing the word "no" on a regular basis. For many, the love expressed in a community of faith or the belief that we are loved as a child of God is enough to get through life's rejections, but since we are prone to take things personally, they can still sting. These excerpted letters are just a couple of the many rejections I have received for scripts written, book proposals shopped, and sermons preached. The feedback from Cary Brokaw and the late Hugh Wilson, both successful movie and TV producers, helped me realize that I should have someone read my sermons before I preach them. I wrote movies for fun, but my livelihood depended on reaching people from the pulpit on a regular basis. Cary and Hugh's thoughtful responses to my movie script had a lasting impact on how I have approached anything I write for public consumption. When even the professionals rewrite up to four times, then we who have the privilege of sharing our thoughts to many constituents should take notice. In a world where multiple messages are thrown at us on a daily basis, it would be reassuring to know that a clergy person took the time to write and, if necessary, revise his or her Saturday or Sunday offering thoughtfully.

Dear Peter, *July 21, 2017*

Seventy-five! Wow! And to think back when we met just a few days after my husband's death in 1981. I feel so blessed that my friends sought you out to be there for me, widowed with Laura at two and a half. Who would have thought we would be married four years later and begin an amazing life together? And here we are now, thirty-five years later, about to celebrate your big seventy-fifth here at the Cape with our family and friends for an evening of bocce and bar-b-cue. You have been and continue to be the most wonderful partner I could ever ask for. You passed the test our first week of dating— starting with our Fourth of July parade and Santa Monica Bay fireworks sail, to the Hollywood Bowl, and then dancing together at Buzzy's birthday bash at the BABC.[22]

Thank you for adding such a wonderful dimension to my life with intellectual conversations about the environment, politics, spiritual insights, exposing me to the art of collecting and preserving what is important, and beyond—to exploring the world with me on some of our special anniversary trips to the Galapagos, Africa, and the Amazon! I can't wait to "dance" with you tonight and for many more years to come. Let the adventure continue and take us wherever it may lead. Happy, happy, birthday! I love you, my Renaissance man!

Katy

Parishioners tend to view clergy spouses as persons who are defined by their public partners; one clergy spouse even introduced herself to me as Mrs. John Smith. Katy, a professional career real estate agent, mother, grandmother, and supportive spouse, has enabled me to become who I am. Teammates are essential in ministry. The lay governing boards, the volunteer guilds that orchestrate worship services, and the multiple committees—from stewardship to outreach—all pale in comparison to the help provided by a spouse who is there as her or his partner exercises their ministry. There is no doubt that the challenges of ministry would have been rough had Katy not walked the path with me for the last thirty-five years. She has defended her liberal, occasionally outspoken, husband during more than one cocktail party attack. Equally important, as my body has suffered the ravages of a few major health issues, she has tolerated my behavioral and mood shifts with grace and patience. We should never forget that placing one's spouse as "Numero Uno" is the right order of priority.

---

[22]Bel-Air Bay Club in Pacific Palisades, California.

Dear Father Peter,

Thank you for baptizing me. Thank you for taking care of the world. Thank you for showing me the communion set.

Natalie Allen, St. Matthew's Parish School

It may come as a surprise to some, but those of us who have spent a lifetime working with children truly appreciate the special gifts we receive from the most vulnerable among us. These young "teachers," including the three-to-five-year-old preschoolers whom I visited every Monday morning for almost twenty years, offered unconditional love and acceptance that carried me through the rest of the week. To receive a permanent expression of thanks like Natalie's note is a treasure that one can savor for a lifetime. Thank you to every student who sat with me in our exploration of the world around us.

Unknowingly, Natalie summed up my ministry in twenty-one succinct words. She covered the sacerdotal functions, my voice for all in God's creation, and the fact that both in chapel and from the pulpit I gave tangible examples to illustrate and explain difficult concepts.

Right on target, Natalie. You are welcome!

Dear Peter,

I look very much forward to:

1. *Meeting your new bride.*
2. *Whipping you in singles.*
3. *Stuffing you in one-on-one [basketball].*
4. *Drinking your beer!*
5. *Catching up with you, my friend.*

   Cheers, George

 The Reverend George Andrews, Headmaster

St. Georges Rhode Island, Saint Andrew's Florida

Dear El Padre,

Greetings from Marion. When does the L.A. Express arrive in H-Port? I am definitely coming to see you—can you guarantee you can teach me to windsurf?

Cheers, Larry[23]

The Reverend George Andrews, Virginia Theological Seminary (VTS) class of '70, was one of the reasons I became a priest. Outgoing, thoughtful, bright, and inclusive, he was also a member of the talented VTS basketball squad of 1969 along with Pittman McGehee, Steve Davenport, Tom Blair, John Hines, Steve Sabom, and me. Many of us had played college basketball, but the teamwork—indeed, the sisterhood and brotherhood aspect of the priesthood—was apparent in our success as a team. In the middle of our third and final year at seminary all fifty-seven of us in our class were asked to sign a declaration of intent towards ordination. I was the only one in my class who did not sign. Two months later, after reflecting upon my classmates, especially Pickett Miles, Mike Vermillion, Jim Sell, and the members of the basketball team, I concluded that I would be proud to be in their company for a lifetime. My decision to join the Episcopal priesthood was deeper than the friendship factor, but these teammates and other classmates were certainly a major reason that I approached Dean Jesse Trotter and said, "Sign me up; I'm ready." George may have said it best when he wrote, "I look forward to catching up with you my friend." I still have not had the opportunity to teach George windsurfing, but 2019 is going to be our year.

---

[23]George signed the letter as "Larry" to pay homage to Larry Bird, the All-Star pro basketball legend.

> THE WHITE HOUSE
> WASHINGTON
>
> We would like to extend our deepest thanks and appreciation for your generous gift.
>
> It is gratifying to know that we have your support. As we work to address the great challenges of our time, we hope you will continue to stay active and involved.
>
> Again, thank you for your kind gift.
>
> *[signatures: Barack Obama, Michelle Obama]*
>
> WWW.WHITEHOUSE.GOV

For more than forty years, I have been collecting historical magazines featuring the United States flag on the cover. I scour thrift stores and eBay for these treasures, often having to purchase a set of magazines in order to get to the one issue that is sporting the flag. As a result, I've acquired a lot of extraneous magazines. One such magazine was titled *Mentor*, an early issue of which featured President Lincoln on the cover. I have always admired Lincoln and consider him, as does our nation collectively, our greatest president.

Shortly after our forty-fourth president, Barack Obama, was elected, I found out that he shared my admiration and respect for Lincoln. I decided to share my chance discovery of this historical magazine with him. I looked up the address of the White House, the simplicity of which made me smile—The White House Washington D.C. 20500. Off went the issue of *Mentor* with a brief explanatory note.

This personally signed (or, most likely, stamped) note arrived about two months later. My takeaway is that a democratic presidency honors the outreach of all citizens. Granted, individual citizens do not have a staff the size of the First Family's, but neither do we receive thousands of letters and requests every week. Sometimes a simple card of thanks, such as this one I received from the Obamas, is all that it takes to reflect the thoughtfulness of the sender.

P.S. President and Mrs. Obama invited me to stay active and involved. These days, I take as a forceful directive their invitation to continue to participate in our nation's unfolding story. I plan to stay involved as long as I am able!

Dear Peter,   *6/20/91*

It is with pleasure and great anticipation that I confirm your appointment as the first Minister to the Environment, Diocese of Los Angeles.

You have my support, and the weight of my office, as you endeavor to create an ongoing task force and program that will benefit the parishes and missions of the diocese, as well as helping to serve as a model for the entire Episcopal Church.

I know that you are presently building "the team," soliciting parish involvement, and formulating strategy that will enable our diocese to take a leadership role in promoting stewardship of creation. Thank you for your commitment, vision, and understanding of a vital, and increasingly important part of the ministry of The Episcopal Church.

Faithfully,

Fred

This succinct letter from the late Right Reverend Frederick H. Borsch, PhD, bishop of the Diocese of Los Angeles, placed my ministry in a context that defines my personal and professional focus to this day.

Without renouncing what the collar represents, I decided to chart my own path and my bishop graciously affirmed my choice. Science and theology are not incompatible. I wear the collar with pride, walk comfortably among environmentalists, and acknowledge science as the core diagnostic and remediation tool in the campaign to preserve the environment. I also firmly believe that without leadership from all levels of the church hierarchy framing the discourse and dialogue, our planet would lose its strongest advocate. Let us always remember that our Judeo-Christian heritage and scripture encourage all human beings to ʻābad and šāmar—Hebrew for *serve and preserve*[24]—creation.

Knowing that someone—whether it be your bishop, your boss, your parent, or a friend—walks with you on your journey and values your contributions is as invaluable as it is reassuring when you are creating and implementing new forms of ministry. Bishop Borsch was always supportive of my work, and I am eternally grateful that I had him in my corner. When the clergy lead, the people will follow.

---

[24] Thanks to Dr. Stephen L. Cook, the Catherine N. McBurney Professor of Old Testament Language and Literature at Virginia Theological Seminary, for proofing my Hebrew translation and transliteration.

Dear Pete,   *Spring 1991*

I have just finished reading your prospectus on Earth Service Inc., and I am impressed. A great deal of thought, experience, and planning has gone into its formation. The thrust is, of course, very noble and I trust your dreams are fulfilled. Much headway is being made to[ward] an awareness of the damage we are causing to the environment, but it will take such energy as yours and your colleagues to put the problems in the spotlight. I trust you will keep us updated.

      Vic Patrone

Mr. Vic Patrone was my father's roommate and fraternity brother at Brown University. They graduated in 1938 and continued to be best of friends throughout their lives. They both would be 103 years old if alive today in 2019. I include his special note of encouragement because I knew Mr. Patrone well and he articulated care about our planet at a time when few others his age expressed their concern.

Mr. Patrone was an all-star collegiate athlete, a champion at his golf club, a student leader, World War II hero, and successful family man and businessman. My dad and his best buddy were both wonderful examples of the Greatest Generation. And because they were of an era when people wrote letters regularly, I have this cherished note of encouragement from a man who was a great role model for any generation.

Dear Peter,

It is wonderful and so important that your show is seen on television. You are bringing out vital environmental issues and discussing them in a forum that is educational, enlightening, inspiring, and not boring! Thank you for all your hard work. I hope more stations will pick up the show.

Best Wishes, Alexandra

I am writing to endorse the show Kaleidoscope. *It is a unique and exciting program. I hope it has an opportunity to continue in its mission to inform and educate a wide audience on the perils and complexities of environmental issues facing the world today. This forum of communicating these issues is essential to gaining strength for the environmental movement. By completing its thirtieth show,* Kaleidoscope *has shown its ability to maintain solid standing and it should continue in its pursuits.*

For the environment, Randy Hayes

Alexandra Paul was my co-host on our TV show *Kaleidoscope/Earth Talk Today*. We taped approximately 190 episodes together. Randy Hayes was one of our most popular and articulate guests. I consider them to be environmental prophets of the twenty-first century. Alexandra, a proponent of zero-population growth, leads by example with a vegan, non-consumption-based lifestyle. Randy, described by the *Wall Street Journal* as "an environmental pit bull," is an advocate for the "lungs of the planet," a co-founder of the think tank Foundation Earth, and the first director of the Rainforest Action Network. In his review of my book *The Earth's Killer C's*, Randy wrote, "Kreitler calls for radical solutions to the ecological carnage," a commentary that captures one of my motivations for leaving parish ministry to serve the earth. Every citizen of planet earth should demonstrate in word and deed their appreciation for the environmentalists and scientists who are the voices for the voiceless—especially our endangered species—worldwide. Clergy of all faiths have a biblical imperative to promote sound stewardship of the ecosystems we have inherited. Saving the planet is the point of intersection that unites the scientific and theological communities. Creating partnerships among environmentalists and clergy should be a high priority for apologists and activists from both disciplines. Perhaps every diocese in The Episcopal Church could begin by putting people like Alexandra and Randy on their vestries and governing boards.

Dear Father Peter,

How wonderful to hear from you! But how typical too. We've lived in nineteen places and must have tested twenty-five different parishes, but this is the first time we've received such a personal note from anybody with whom we've had such fleeting contact. When we sell this house, we'll move to Kansas to be near our kids—but it looks as though it is going to take ages.

We hope you had a merry and blessed Christmas and that the new year will be happy and rewarding.

Sincerely,

Hal and Laura Ellsworth

While communities of faith value long-term participation, this gracious thank-you note underscores the importance of being kind to all who arrive at the church's doorstep, even if it is just for a short time. I can't recall what type of career compelled the Ellsworth family to move so often, but I am glad I reached out to them.

I am always on the lookout for patterns in peoples' lives, especially negative repetitive behavior. What does it say about the church that none of the many other parishes they had attended or tried out had followed up with a personal note? My modus operandi with newcomers is to reach out and offer a hand; after all, the way that a community of faith greets people says a lot about how welcoming and supportive an environment it will be. My correspondence with the Ellsworths showcases just how much it can mean to newcomers to receive a personal letter.

Dear Rev. Peter Kreitler   *3/18/87*

Thank you for your thoughtful and perceptive column in today's L.A. Times. *As the author of a recently published book entitled* Salvation for Sale, *which chronicles my time spent working for [TV evangelist] Pat Robertson, I fully understand your concerns. I applaud your taking a stand and speaking out because the dangers are real—and if you were to read my book you might find out just how dangerous the televangelists really are.*

Peace,

Gerard Thomas Straub

The fact that this gentleman had worked for a TV evangelist emboldened me all the more to raise my voice regarding the distortion of the gospels in my time. I admire individuals who speak truth to power; they are rare because many people are afraid to speak up or speak out. Writers' words last an eternity, and clergy have a golden opportunity every week to offer substantive commentary on the scriptures. My few attempts at spreading my understanding of truth through the press have helped define who I am. Confronting the powers that be may result in condemnation and ridicule in the short-term, but building a platform upon which others may stand in the future is part of our calling as clergy.

Today, more than at any time in my seventy-seven years on the planet and almost fifty years as a priest, my concern about religion being co-opted by the state, by specific politicians, and by clergy is at its zenith. We must always speak up and speak out. In the United States of America, there is no such thing as a national religion.

Thank you, Mr. Straub, you were prophetic in your book *Salvation for Sale.*

Dearest Peter,

It has been three months since I called you, unable to breathe. I have thanked you over and over in my mind and heart—it is about time I thanked you in person.

I don't think I've ever had a moment like that before—the wind was just completely knocked out of my sails. You were there, and I can't tell you how much it meant to me to hear your voice, feel your care, follow your guidance. It was the essence of crisis intervention and I will never forget it.

Much has changed and gone unchanged since that day, of course. I am feeling good and strong right now—I hope it lasts. Please know that if you ever can't breathe, I'm here too.

Thank You.

With love,

Barbie

Most people won't ever know how busy or preoccupied an actively engaged priest may be because of the delicacy and confidentiality with which many pastoral emergencies must be handled. Priests have to be very nimble on their feet because calls that come in at all hours of the day and night often redirect activities in an instant. Even a routine trip to the market can turn into a pastoral emergency. I was once in our local Gelson's Market and paramedics came rushing in to attend to a parishioner of mine who had passed out just one aisle away from me.

Thankfully, all Episcopal priests undergo crisis training during their seminary years. I spent an entire summer in Clinical Pastoral Education under the tutelage of chaplain David Wyatt at Overlook Hospital in Summit, New Jersey. Priests are not expected to be back-up doctors, but a pastoral visit can truly soothe those who are suffering. Some churches employ specialists in pastoral care because of the frequency with which clergy are called to respond to parishioners in need.

As clergy, we are called to show up. Sometimes the outcome is good; other times the most support we can provide is simply being present to help shepherd another person through times of loss and sadness. Barbie's letter, which meant a lot to me, reinforced my belief that simply hearing another person's familiar voice can make a big difference to those who are in distress.

Dear Rev. Kreitler,   *March 12, 1981*

I have just finished "How to Prevent an Affair" in the March issue of Redbook *magazine. It is excellent! And how I wish I could use it as a basis to pull my marriage back together. This is the situation: My husband announced that he is gay after twenty-five years of married life and two sons, that he wanted to stay married (for the children's sake, financial, appearances, etc. I think), but that he needed to be free to live his own life and be with his friends (gay, I imagine) without restriction or resentment from me. He does not believe this is contrary to the marriage commitment. The emotional trauma that I have lived with has been indescribable for over a year, trying to keep our home going for our two sons as well as a tenuous relationship with my husband. What would Christ have me do in this situation? is the big question I face and no answer seems forthcoming.*

I still love my husband very much. I have searched the scriptures and find that Jesus does not touch directly on this question. I say your words of wisdom to married couples is excellent. It is very reassuring to see this type of book written by a minister from a Christian point of view.

Sincerely,

[Name Withheld]

Many well-meaning, religious, or spiritually-inclined individuals succumb to the human temptation of adultery. Sadly, the pain and guilt are often compounded by sanctimonious proclamations from the pulpit. I believe that a preventive regimen within a marriage may reduce the chances of an extramarital affair and thus spare people the pain that infidelity causes. There is a caveat, however, when a spouse chooses a same-sex partner. People tend to internalize all manner of guilt or self-doubt and wonder what they could have done differently to keep the marriage intact. In fact, there is little one could have done to save a marriage in situations where a partner leaves due to his or her sexual orientation. Some clergy exacerbate the already difficult situation when their first reaction is to judge a person based on sexual orientation.

Homosexuality is nothing new; it has been as entrenched, though not as accepted, in cultures throughout history as heterosexuality. Clerical leaders would be wise to step back and lead with compassion and understanding rather than condemnation. Those in the helping professions must be sensitive when the adultery commandment is broken, regardless of sexual preferences. First and foremost, be kind, as Christ would have been. Remember that Christ never condemned homosexuality nor is it called out in the Ten Commandments.

Dear Rev. Kreitler,   *2/22/81*

I just read your article [in the latest issue of Redbook*] on avoiding an affair. I'm going to keep it handy for a reminder, but the prevention part is too late. I'm the one who had an affair and am still trying to get over the affair and rebuild my marriage.*

The man I fell in love with was the youth minister at my church. I was running the church school at the time so we spent hours working together. He was new to the community and the church; I had been there for twenty years. I was Episcopalian; he was not. At the time I was forty-three and he was thirty-four. I was married, the mother of three teenagers, one of whom was in the youth group; he was a bachelor. We had many things in common and enjoyed each other immensely. I had never been in love before and it was wonderful for both of us. We were together for four months of real joy and then he decided it must end and stopped seeing me completely—without saying a word to me. I was totally miserable and my husband found out because of my misery, so he was miserable too. But my lover and I would not stay apart and for another year we lived together on and off again. An affair with hell at home. Finally, things got so bad I took an overdose of pills and spent six weeks in the psych ward with a nervous breakdown. When I went back to church, it was as if I didn't exist to my former lover. Then, after two months we started seeing each other again. Again, after several months he decided we must part and proceeded to do everything he could to make me miserable. Finally, I couldn't take it any longer and left the church. That was almost two years ago and we've only spoken once and that briefly and in a store. During all this, my husband and I fought it out and worked out many problems. Somewhere in there I got my master's degree and became a librarian and a working wife. When we left our church, we were very bitter. The rector had not been willing to help; in fact, I think he was glad to see us go. Nothing like having a real-life sinner in your church! After searching the city for a new church, we have settled in at [redacted] Church. They welcomed us with such love and joy! When we were going to join, I talked to the minister about why we had left our former church. He was very nonjudgmental. Because we parted in such anger and hurt, I have written to my former lover and asked for his forgiveness and given him mine; he never responded.

I can't even begin to tell you what a horrible and painful experience this has all been. My husband and I have worked out an amicable relationship. We've been married twenty-six years now. That's a lot of history together to cast aside. I have no feelings for him beyond any affection born out of that history. I never desired him sexually and had never even known what passion and desire was like until I fell in love. As soon as I left [my lover] for good, I went back to no sexual desire. I seem to have lost all my ability to feel anything— joy or sorrow—yet sometimes I long to live for someone and to feel love again. I feel like such a hypocrite in church. What if they knew why we were there? Would they still want me? I listen to the lessons and wonder about things like not going to the altar if you have anything against your brother, forgiving each other, all those wonderful sermons I grew up on and believed. [My lover] never even came to see me in the hospital. He didn't say a word when I left his church even though he knew it was the center of my life. Sometimes I am full of hatred toward him and other times I miss him so much—it's a physical pain. My husband and I don't see each other very much—we are both very busy. Sometimes I get so lonely I want to call my lover and beg him to take me back no matter what, but I never do; I'm not a total masochist.

Our children are all out on their own now—in fact we have grandchildren. I am forty-eight now and the road ahead looks endless and very lonely. Thank you for listening. If you have any suggestions, I certainly would like to hear them.

Sincerely,

"Jane Doe"

Preventing an affair is easier than dealing with the aftermath, but this anonymous woman asked for suggestions, so here they are:

1. Ask for and demand respect for your feelings.
2. Seek out a supportive counselor who is a good listener. Ask for a thirty-minute intake interview before selection. Getting help for yourself is essential, regardless of the eventual outcome.
3. Try to avoid gossiping about your unfaithful partner.
4. Blaming God, the church, or others hurts your chances for reconciliation or healing.
5. Rebuilding self-esteem in the wake of an affair can take a long time, but counseling can help both parties to recognize their inherent value.
6. A "woe is me" attitude is, while understandable, not constructive.

In addition, one of experts on whom I relied, Dr. Anthony Rosenthal, commented in *Affair Prevention*, "the affair may be a way of acting out an internal personal problem, and under these circumstances it may not threaten the marriage." My advice is to wait until you really understand what is going on with your spouse before you take any drastic actions.

Current statistics state that one-half of all marriages will face the issue of adultery. One might then presume that fifty percent of the couples in one's congregation will be in need of pastoral care that is loving, supportive, and nonjudgmental.

We do not learn from experience; we learn from reflecting upon our experiences.
   The Reverend Richard A. Busch PhD

Dear Peter,

Things are quiet here at Casa Con Ed. The quiet is welcome for me—a welcome change. I find I can handle all that rather well if I get out and have some contact with people at lunchtime.

A personal word—It was a treat to be with you in the group this summer. Being a witness to the growth, struggle, clarity, and movement in your life is a privilege. Hang in there with your reading and discussing. That kind of change comes for me in such fits and starts, so I need to hang in there with others who will hang in there with me.

Special love to you and your friend,

    Fondly,

    Dick

The Reverend Richard A. Busch, PhD was the director of the Center for Continuing Education[25] at Virginia Theological Seminary. He became a mentor and friend, and our relationship was cemented when I participated in a three-week continuing education program in 1990. His wisdom was both readily apparent and timeless. Time and again I find myself referencing and passing on his lessons. I'm particularly reminded of his counsel to remember, "We do not learn from experience, we learn from reflecting upon our experiences."

Thanks to Dr. Busch, reflection became a pillar of my theology. This letter, which I reread thirty-four years after I received it, reminded me of his wisdom. Dick encouraged me to continue my reading, writing, and discussions—another tripod upon which I have built my career as a priest.

---

[25]Now part of the Lifelong Learning program.

Dear Reverend Kreitler,

I enjoyed our meeting but have thought since that perhaps I could have opened the door to a more frank exchange. Those very nice young people were, of course, being polite to an invited guest. I should have realized they would be and, therefore, would perhaps refrain from asking questions that might have seemed blunt or even a touch hostile. I regret I didn't say this and urge them to ask whatever question might be on their minds. Sometimes those are the best questions, and sometimes the answer clears up a possible misunderstanding. Again, thanks and best regards,

Ronald Reagan

Being respectful of people who are in the public spotlight comes naturally when you happen to minister in a town where celebrities and famous people reside. Nancy and Ronald Reagan lived in Pacific Palisades at the time of the 1980 presidential election. Shortly after Mr. Reagan won that election, I quietly invited Mrs. Reagan to speak to our young couples' club. We thought she might enlighten us about what it was like to be a governor's wife and soon-to-be First Lady. A week before she was scheduled to speak at our club gathering, her secretary called and said, "Mrs. Reagan regrets she has to cancel but asks, 'would you mind if Ronnie came?'" After I had fallen out of my chair, I regained my cool and replied, "Sure, that would be fine." In early January, President-elect Reagan—accompanied by three secret servant agents—knocked on the door, settled in a big easy chair, and talked with a dozen of us for over two hours. He was charming and engaging—he leaned forward in his chair when speaking—and even tried out several ideas for his inaugural address.

The content of the character of this gentleman president comes through in this personal letter that he wrote following our meeting. The man who was about to become the busiest and most powerful person on the planet took the time to write a personal note. What a lesson for all of us, especially when we think we are too busy to write a letter to communicate our appreciation, condolences, or support.

Dear Sir,

Re: Your article in the L.A. Times

I have long wanted to write someone about some real concerns I have about "religion" in America and the clergy. It regards the religious leaders and organizations as well as local churches...As Jesus spread His word in the manner of some in his day, I think the religious leaders and organizations have to do the same...the manner today is not only the pulpit but also the printed media and the TV...

I have found also a prevalence in the regular "church-going Christians" of...self-righteousness, judgmental attitudes of downright nastiness while quoting the Bible as the absolute word of God, according to their beliefs, and apparently not being taught in their churches that their own personal behavior in day-to-day life should be guided by the teachings of Jesus. My complaint and concern are that the Christian organizations and leaders and local clergy have done nothing to change this. Because you did write the article, I am hoping you belong to some type of leadership and will urge them to speak out publicly to combat this trend of self-righteous intolerance...

*I feel a great deal of emphasis should be made on making moral judgment on oneself, not judging others. Jesus didn't organize to combat the moral behavior of the people nor to combat the questionable behavior of the church and government leaders. He taught the people what their own behavior should be. It is the self-righteous, apparently ego-inspired attitude so often encountered in the churchgoer—they are right and if you don't agree with them, you don't believe in God, or sometimes you aren't even good Americans. I feel also the churches, in teaching the Bible, fail to relate the teachings to current everyday life. When did you ever hear the church speak out against anything the rich and famous do? Stealing and lying and government and politicians—along with business practices—**the clergy has sure played hands off with these basics**...**My point in all this is that I wish the clergy would take some courageous stands and then emphasize them.***

Signed,

[Name Withheld]

P.S. Please do not use my name for anything—This letter denies you that right, for personal reasons.

This is a heavily redacted version of what I believe is the longest letter I ever received in my career, but my response is simple and direct. I wish more people of faith gave their religion as much thought as this individual does. I took her advice to heart and hopefully other clergy will as well.

My dear Father Kreitler,   *3/18/87*

I read your article this morning with interest. My points are

> *1. I have an off button on my TV. I am not required by law, conscience, or intimidation to watch any religious program.*

> *2. The Lord commanded us to preach the gospel in all the world. Can you think of a more efficient way to reach more people than TV?*

> *3. The first thing the Communists do when taking over a country is to persecute the church.*

> *4. As for borderline theology—is yours the only theology? Or mine? Or the [electronic preachers]? The only true theology is Christ's.*

> *5. You are free to have your own TV program. Then you can freely preach against the intolerance of others. I enjoyed the caption of your article.*

> *6. The electronic church has brought thousands and thousands to the saving knowledge of Christ. Can any one preacher do that from his limited pulpit?*

Sincerely, [Name Withheld]

P.S. I'm an Episcopalian. May the Lord bless you and keep you.

This is an excerpt of a letter I received after my article, "TV Preachers' Religious Intolerance Can't Be Tolerated," appeared in the *Los Angeles Times* editorial section on March 18, 1997. Here is my point-by-point response to my fellow Episcopalian:

> 1. I agree.

> 2. TV is efficient, but not very personal.

> 3. The church in our democratic nation is not infallible, and it should not be exempt from legitimate concerns about how it operates.

> 4. Theology is the study of God. Christianity is one of many religions that worship God.

> 5. I am well aware that television is a medium that can be used for good. In the 1970s I hosted a television program for teens and adults that addressed drug abuse. In the 1990s I hosted my second television program, this time focusing on environmental issues.

> 6. Watching television will never be a substitute for attending a local community of faith, as one is able. I must add the caveat that housebound adults might benefit from hearing "the Word" preached via the airwaves.

I have found that one's lifestyle and consumption patterns reveal a lot about one's character. I try not to judge too harshly; none of us, including clergy, are perfect or exempt from sin.

Mr. Kreitler,   *3/18/87*

"We have three enemies, the world, the flesh, and the devil." Most of you expert religionists never refer to any of them. Instead you throw rocks at those who do take a stand. It's popular now to criticize and damn the conservative right, to lambast everything from Reagan to religion.

P.S. I get more theology from one TV man than I do from nine of you in a local pulpit. Sorry about that!

Signed,

"Roger A."

Here is another letter I received in response to my op-ed piece. Roger's criticism begins with calling me an expert religionist and one who is prone to throwing rocks. I am neither. However, speaking truth about my chosen profession while I promote its role in our culture is part of my understanding of my job description.

Roger claims he benefits nine-fold from one TV personality as opposed to those who serve local congregations. Granted, megachurches have proliferated since the 1990s and reach millions,[26] but pastors must never be granted an exemption from accountability. Lifestyle and spending choices may be a good measure of a preacher's credibility. Whether her or his words from the pulpit match behavior—or there is a Rolls Royce in the driveway and a jet at the local airport—may speak volumes about their priorities.

Recognizing that all humans—including clergy of all faiths—fall short of the mark, I still find strength in the local congregations, mosques, or synagogues of our nation. When a preacher offers commentary on the scripture, current events, or controversial issues to a live audience that she or he sees week after week, a level of trust and openness can be fostered to everyone's benefit. Plus, local congregations—where most clergy exercise their ministries—have governing boards, elders, or vestries that provide checks and balances. A hierarchy of authority is not a perfect solution but, like the prophets of old who held up mirrors that reflected the behavior of the people—especially the rich and powerful—these boards inject added transparency and accountability into the equation. The advice is clear: never throw rocks, but avoid looking the other way when there is egregious distortion of the truth.

---

[26] A megachurch is defined as any Protestant church having an average weekend attendance of two thousand or more people. In 2010, the Hartford Institute for Religion Research database listed 1,300 megachurches in the United States.

Dear Fr. Kreitler,

I read your article in the Episcopal News *tonight, and thought, if only I had known about you three years ago before I plunged into an affair. I would not today be in that affair and so deeply in love with no way to satisfy that love because we both are married, and he will not consider divorce, although I would not hesitate to do so now.*

At the time I begged for help with our clergyman, with my husband (who promised but never followed through), and even with a local counseling center (twice). Everyone's answer was the same: "we don't know how to help you." The problem was impotency. It still is. Anyway, I wanted to write and express how I feel about your ideas on affairs.

Sincerely,

[Name Withheld]

One six-word phrase from this letter stands out: "we don't know how to help you." Though not directed at me, I took the writer's comment personally. It exposed something that was lacking in my education, clinical pastoral education, and experience. In response, I dedicated myself to continuing education and to building a network of other specialists on the continuum of care.

Consider the following situation I found myself in back in 1977: a person shares that he or she is wrestling with their sexuality by dating both men and women. I thought to myself, Did we discuss this scenario in seminary? Was I comfortable dealing with the issue? I knew not to wing it before I talked to an expert. When I found myself immersed in situations that required a skillset that was above my pay grade, I sought the counsel and advice of others or referred folks to my "go-to team" of experts who were better trained and suited to help. Especially in cases in which I felt a drug or alcohol interdiction was warranted, I would call "Dr. Jones" or "therapist Smith" who had strong credentials in the field. Cultivating relationships with other experts and being willing to ask for help are some of the hallmarks of a successful person.

The bottom line is to be a compassionate clergy person. Be an active listener. Engage the person who is asking for help with both ears, both eyes, and an alert posture that indicates interest. It is OK not to always have the answers, but it is not OK to push people away or make stuff up. Quoting Bible passages or offering words like "God loves you" are not substitutes for doing one's homework. We cannot help everyone, but we can build a procedural pattern so that—through our pastoral presence, proactive counsel, and referrals—the individual feels that God *does* love them.

Peter,

It appears that we are approaching new beginnings and I am very excited for you. Even though I don't have to write, I wanted you to know you are a very meaningful and positive force for those who know you. Your contributions to St. Matthew's are far too many to even attempt to list.

You have truly made a difference for those in time of grief and have been a shelter to give relief. While we cannot be everything to everyone, you have walked the upper path and did not succumb to the pedestrian trivialities. I have enjoyed the time we have shared together and look forward to many more years. I may even join Greenpeace. Don't ever change—there is only one P.K. and we would sorely miss you.

Buster

It just may be that my all-time favorite personal affirmation came from the same friend who gave me a book about Toltec wisdom and The Four Agreements.[27] The second of those agreements is not to take anything, whether negative or positive, personally. Buster, known more for his humor than his ability to provide memorable quotes, made my day when he wrote, "you have walked the upper path and did not succumb to pedestrian trivialities."

Since we are all fallible, I imagine that my version of walking the upper path is not quite the same as the straight and narrow path, but is instead a metaphor for doing the best I can to act ethically and with integrity and honesty along my life journey. Buster's late lovely wife Sharon was a seeker of truth. She always pushed me to explore all religions and philosophies and she remained a disciple—a learner—to the end of her days. Buster continues her legacy of exploration and walks in Sharon's upper path, as should we all. It is not our job as clergy to prescribe the path, but we can give people some of the tools to chart a course to their own truth.

---

[27] The Toltecs are an indigenous people of Mexico. In his 1997 book *The Four Agreements,* Don Miguel Ruiz examines life principles distilled from the Toltec tradition.

> Dear Mr. Kreitler, can you possibly read the May 25, 1988 new book, "AIDS" & THE DRS. OF DEATH, by Dr. AlanCantwellJrM You cannot believe what sort of info is caontained in it. Well, we sure can see how the fundies are handling "AIDS" as God's divine wrath. What is really spooky is to know that fundies, as in the DRUG LORD Jim Jones, may not even know how much they are being controlled by neo-nazi elements. Have you ever watche the things on TBN which are so GERMANe to this question of fundy salvation through the bornagainers experiences of walking in fire, speaking in tongues, and POWERS of spiritual discernment in whic the holy ghost imparts revelations? We hope you see exactly what is so GERMANe on TrinityBroadcastingNetwork! Perhaps you will see Paul Crouch iscuss his heritage, as only an American might! We love the POWERMEN for Christ, and the displays of God muscl le men who are such good and able Christian soldiers. Now how do you see the Guardian Angels as a potential conditioning process? And what about Gen. Singlaub and his band of merry bornagain paramilitarymen playing war games in foothills ofAmerica? And wha sort of DRUG LORDS are in West Hollywood, nearD nny'sDogs on SantaMonicaBlvd. Try the ULTIMATE EVIL by MauryTerry and see whence arises satanism and DRUG LORDS! TheCRIMES OF PATRIOT should be collated, too. See the FIRST AIDS epidemics as real aids What sort of psy-terror warfare of '1984' "AIDS" and subconscious arrousals when you HEAR aids, aides, and AYDS, and AIDS. AYDS is changing its name to AYDSLIM to boost sales! ha, ha, ha Why was the OCBUSINESSJOURNAL investigating TBN, CH40????????

I received this anonymous "best use of space" postcard in 1988, well after the Acquired Immune Deficiency Syndrome (AIDS) epidemic was in full force. I'm sad to say that the church's reaction to the crisis was mixed—even in The Episcopal Church—and some clergy viciously blamed the homosexual community for the spread of the disease in the United States. The story played out in my congregation in two ways. Many in our parish refused to take communion from the common cup for fear of catching the disease. They would dip the bread or host in the wine, but would never accept the chalice itself. We tried to explain that the virus that causes AIDS is not transmitted by saliva, but the distinction fell on deaf ears in those first few years. I also took a confidential call one day from a person in the parish who felt such guilt that he had to share his story. He had had a sexual fling while on location filming a movie and had contracted the deadly disease. His health deteriorated rapidly, and a month later, I was called to his bedside where he asked for extreme unction—his final anointing—the first and only request of its kind that I ever received. His remorse over cheating on his spouse was so intense that he cried out for help. The formal rite of forgiveness I could offer that day was powerful and healing. He died shortly thereafter.

Dear Peter and Katy, May 6, 1997

Thanks for your kind and touching letter. I appreciate all your good work, but also your agonizing over the path.

I'm back in Sacramento fighting for the Endangered Species Act against the odds. The message is simple: no permits for incidental or accidental "take" unless there is a net benefit for endangered species and habitat.

In addition, I'm working to fulfill promises made in the mayor's race: hiring inner-city staff for a peace process, getting budget funds for the L.A. River, building a community college service corps in public schools etc.

Let me know how I can be of service—especially as you acolyte in matters eco-spiritual.

Sincerely,

Tom

Senator Tom Hayden

Unlike Catholic priests, Episcopal clergy are allowed to marry and have families. I wanted to include one letter addressed to both Katy and me because I would not have enjoyed the career that I have had were it not for the support of my spouse. We often think of doctors, lawyers, and politicians as having time-consuming jobs, but clergy also face challenging demands on their time. Maintaining a balance between career and family is not always easy. Katy was always supportive, first as I served as a parish priest, then when I transitioned my ministry to being the diocesan minister to the environment, and then on to my work with Virginia Theological Seminary and the national Episcopal Church on environmental issues and programming.

The late Tom Hayden was a prominent and outspoken voice for the environment and for justice. He also meant it when he said something like "Let me know if I can be of service." Tom walked the talk and was of service to many, myself included, throughout his life. His letter echoes my firmly held belief that preserving the gift of creation for future generations is as much a calling from God as is serving as a parish minister or a military or hospital chaplain or performing social work on behalf of the poor. What's more, he rightfully acknowledged Katy as my partner in that calling.

Kreit:

For God's sake, for Pete's sake, for Christ's sake take good care of yourself. No? Si! For Loomis' sake, for Brown's sake, etc. eat veggies! Soy or rice milk. Save your precious self, father.

You're out there saving everybody else; you dun forgot number one, UNO. One in one hundred restaurants (hold the salad dressing; bring me lemons) has food we should be eating. So yeah, I'm worried about you. Sweat profusely for twenty min. a day, at minimum. You are gifted, gifted with a great body—the cathedral of thyself. So Kreit, hold the course. Eat grass (wheat variety). Get a juicer, if you ain't got one. I wish you very, very well buddy. Take the time you need.

Much love,

Peter

The only person on the planet who calls me "Kreit" is my senior-year roommate at the Loomis School, Peter Barton "Nighthorse" Cummings. Peter, a remarkably gifted athlete, scholar, and artist, once wrote me to pay attention to the plight of Native Americans. His passion for and commitment to our First Nation people brought the issue to my attention. Today his Native American-style art, especially his feather paintings, illustrate his life-long commitment.

Peter had just learned that I was diagnosed with mantle cell lymphatic cancer. His unforgettable letter—written in a style that is particular to good friends—offers both practical and spiritual advice and is illustrative of his care for me. I took his recommendations to heart. At his suggestion, I embraced tofu and seaweed and have tried to maintain a healthy lifestyle as cancer continues to do its dance in my system.

Friendship is a gift. As we can all attest, it's not always easy to maintain, but it's worth the effort. The key word for me is reciprocity. Our fast paced, instant-gratification world slows down for us when we take time to communicate with people we care about and love—and when that love and care are returned, we are blessed!

Dear Peter,   *April 2, 1993*

The Festival of Life weekend has taken hold of this parish in a very significant way this year. High among the many reasons for this deep impact in the lives of people was the quality of the workshop you presented on "Making the Connection: Every Action I Take, Every Decision I Make Has an Environmental Consequence." People have let me and the committee know how their lives have been enriched by your careful and thoughtful work. Please know how deeply grateful the parish and I are to you for sharing your considerable gifts and skills with us.

I appreciate your being with us, especially as the topic is so difficult to engage people on.

Sincerely,

George

The Reverend Canon George Regas, a former rector of the progressive, prestigious All Saints Church in Pasadena, California, was one of my early heroes of The Episcopal Church, along with Presiding Bishop John Hines, Virginia Theological Seminary Dean Jesse Trotter, and the Reverend William Sloane Coffin.[28]

Throughout his distinguished career, he lived up to what I believed to be the high calling of the office. An outstanding preacher, he used his voice during his long and illustrious career to focus on human rights and justice. George's legacy remains a beacon in The Episcopal Church. He is an illuminating example of what a priest can be—and frankly, should be—a person who will shine a bright light on important issues of the day.

I have had the privilege of speaking at secular and faith gatherings about the issue of creation collapsing. To receive the praise of a person I have respected and admired throughout my forty-nine-year career is both humbling and gratifying. Personal notes from busy, engaged agents of change are rare and unexpected and may be another factor in their success.

---

[28] As an aside—I had the honor of having a job interview with Dr. Regas on the campus of VTS in 1969.

> **NATIONAL GALLERY OF ART**
> *Office of the Director*
>
> 5.5.15
>
> Dear Peter and Katy,
>
> Wonderful to see you on your anniversary and very much appreciate seeing what you are up to. Congrats! What about visiting Washington w/ inspiring a cleanup of the Potomac? Hope we can see each other again sooner rather than later.
>
> All best,
>
> [signature]

Rusty Powell was instrumental in the effort to have the Kreitler 1776 Patriotic Magazine Collection featured at the Smithsonian Museum of American History following the attacks on September 11, 2001. Katy and I had the privilege of getting to know Rusty and his wife, Nancy, when he was director of the Los Angeles County Museum of Art, and remained in touch when he took the prestigious job at the National Gallery in Washington, DC. Their Alexandria, Virginia home was once the residence of Robert E. Lee, and their exquisite restoration demonstrated both taste and reverence for classic design.

As we age, many of our acquaintances rise to a level of importance in a variety of fields, but success should be measured by content of character and not just by the title on the door. Mr. Earl "Rusty" Powell is a success by both of these metrics. His humor, intellect, and engagement with everyone he meets is evident in this personal letter that he took time to write despite his busy schedule. I never did take him up on his suggestion of creating a Potomac River cleanup to mirror what we had done in Los Angeles, but I did take to heart his mentoring of me in the art world—as I have tried to do with others in my field.

Dear Peter,   *Feb. 1993*

Here is something that may be of interest to you. You may have noticed the recent increased concern being voiced about immigrants and what they are doing to America, and California, and what they are costing us, and how it is that they will affect our environment. Usually this goes along with calls for more enforcement of current restrictions on immigration and more restrictions.

    Joe

Twenty-six years ago, my friend Joe wrote to engage me in the debate that still polarizes our nation today: immigration. Unless one is descended from native people, each one of us Americans has a lineage that originated somewhere else. Our great nation has become who she is by accepting and assimilating diverse religions, races, and cultures since the boats began to arrive at Jamestown, Virginia in 1607 and Plymouth, Massachusetts in 1620.

Given our nation's history, you would think it would be a foregone conclusion that our communities of faith welcome all people. Fighting for the rights of all immigrants should be the American way since their contributions, across all sectors, has made our nation great. Sadly, Joe was prescient in his alarmist commentary. While I am relieved to see that more and more of our congregations are diverse and inclusive, I continue to pay heed to Joe's prophetic concern. It bears repeating; the future of America depends upon the continued building of bridges, not walls.

April 26, 2012

Hi Peter,

I talked to Sherri about this and she is just as delighted and blown away by your generous offer as I am. We are very honored to be able to offer an incentive like this to encourage pastors to raise the consciousness of their congregations about these huge issues. **We are way behind the curve on this already, and pastors need to be so much more proactive. It is mainly the lay people who are making the changes in local churches.** *I can't tell you how excited we are about the opportunity to do this. An incentive like this and a little competition seems to bring about positive results. At the very least, it will get pastors thinking about the issue more than they have been.*

Blessings, Margaret

Dear Margaret and Sherri,

I would like to remain anonymous. I would also like to call this the Henke-Loveland Environmental Preaching Award, or some such title. You two have been the driving force behind OCICE[29] and I would like to keep your name out in front of all this. The sermons could be sent to me electronically; clergy would assume I am the judge and not associate me with the prize. Open to any other thoughts.

Hugs, Peter

I believe that a primary mission of all clergy—frankly, of all adults—is to help others discover their personal gifts. After OCICE invited me to be its inaugural speaker, I reached out to Margaret and Sherri with the idea of developing a sermon contest. The idea was to use the contest in order to inspire clergy of all denominations to use their homiletic skills to raise awareness about critical issues, especially regarding the environment.

Margaret echoed my experience when she said, "lay people are making the changes" regarding the environment. When the laity lead, the clergy should pay attention and follow their example. Margaret and Sherri are great leaders who are fostering awareness about the changes that individuals and communities of faith can make to protect planet Earth.

---

[29]Orange County Interfaith Coalition for the Environment

...the Earth is secure in the timeless ever-changing path on which God set it. Not so?

Charlton Heston

Dear Peter,   5/8/91

I share your environmental concerns. We use solar power, avoid pollution, recycle what we can...I've even gotten a paper shredder to recycle more effectively the tide of paper that flows through our house. Personally, I am convinced that the most crucial environmental concern is overpopulation. If we don't solve this, all other effort is pointless.

I'm offended though, by the fallacy that this entirely laudable effort is intended to "save the earth." What you're talking about is saving mankind, a good idea but not nearly so selfless...I can understand your concern, as a Christian priest, with saving man as a species, as well as his individual soul. Surely, the Earth is secure in the timeless ever-changing path on which God set it. Not so?

As Ever,

Chuck

This thoughtful note from Charlton "Chuck" Heston is testimony to the fact that it is possible for people on both sides of an issue to listen respectfully and to find wisdom in the viewpoints of another. Lydia and Charlton Heston, an iconic Hollywood couple, lived in a sprawling ranch-style home overlooking the San Fernando Valley in Southern California. In the center of the home was a library containing thousands of books. It was circular in shape, with a wooden ladder on a track that enabled access to the upper levels. Chuck was well read and was conversationally adept on many subjects. I was a guest in his home, debated with him on the couch in his living room, baptized his grandson Jack, and marveled at his relationship with his wife Lydia. We did not always agree on issues of the day, as this letter illustrates, but we engaged each other from a place of knowledge. Chuck and I always seemed to find areas of understanding and acceptance. I have learned that, with patience, we can overcome even the most challenging of political differences. If we take the time to understand the legitimate theological and philosophical lenses through which others view the world, we can understand better how they arrive at their policy positions, even if they are different from ours.

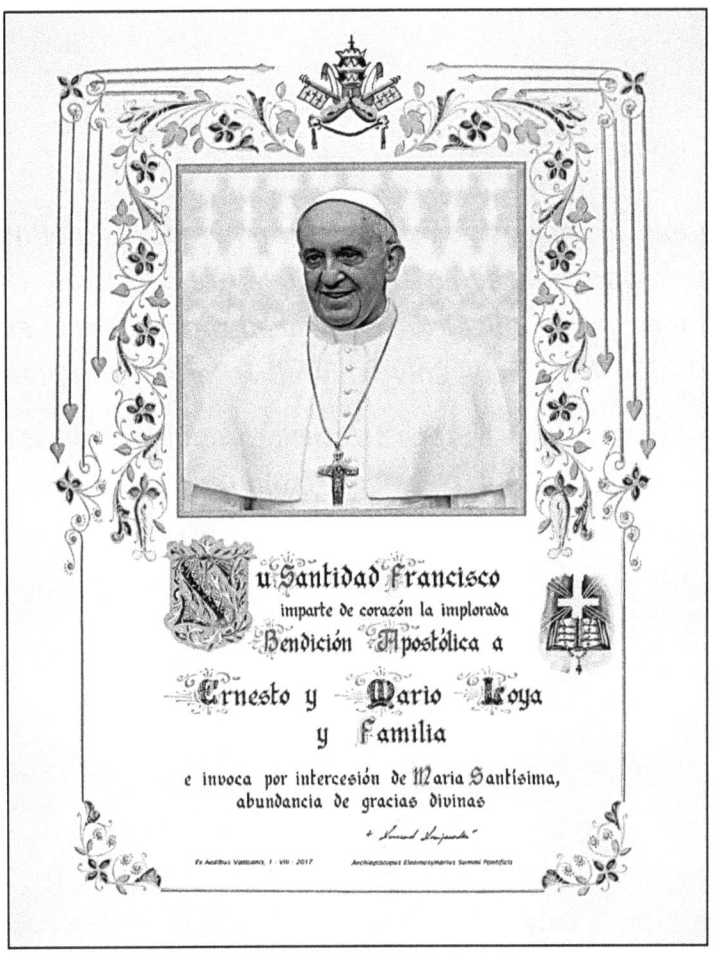

In 2017 I accepted an invitation from friend and colleague John Quigley to join fifty other people to visit Canyon de Guadalupe in Mexico. It became obvious why John dreamed of saving this Garden of Eden–like oasis from development. Warm and cold water flowed from the mountains to create natural pools, and magnificent blue palm trees formed mini cathedrals throughout the property. For my contribution, I offered to write Pope Francis and ask for a Papal Blessing for the Ernesto and Mario Loya family, who have been custodians of the property for over seventy years. Good luck, I thought to myself. I had no idea if it was even possible, but the collaboration between VTS Dean Ian Markham and Vice President for Institutional Advancement Linda Dienno, as well as their connections to the Anglican-Roman Catholic Consultation in Rome, turned my idea and letter into a reality. The Papal Blessing was joyfully received by the Loya family and contributed to their decision not to sell the property to the developers and to offer John and his partners the opportunity to put it into a land trust to be preserved in its wild state forever. Just think, the vision shared by John and his friends became a reality due to a single letter multiplied by providence, personal connections, and the generosity of Pope Francis. Perhaps Canyon de Guadalupe will become the Lourdes of the West?

Dear Peter,   *1/2/18*

It is so lovely to see the Environmental Fund grow. You were ahead of the curve on this one; you were the one who saw the dangers of environmental neglect, decades before others. You have been a prophet for the speechless plants, trees, rivers, mountains, and oceans. It has been a ministry of massive significance.

Yours in gratitude for your friendship,

Ian

The Very Reverend Dean Ian Markham

Virginia Theological Seminary

A few years ago, I had the privilege of attending the inaugural worship service in the recently completed LEED gold-standard-certified, Robert Stern chapel at Virginia Theological Seminary (VTS). The original 1881 church, which I attended when I was a seminarian, burned to the ground in 2010. The beauty of the new worship space is awe-inspiring.

Standing alongside the Dean at the altar that day were the Presiding Bishop of The Episcopal Church Michael B. Curry and former presiding bishops the Right Reverend Frank T. Griswold III and the Right Reverend Katharine J. Schori. The preacher on the momentous occasion was the 105th Archbishop of Canterbury, Justin Welby. It was indeed a diverse all-star cast.

Weaving a creation or environmental ethic into the fabric of the church curriculum will empower men and women of the clergy to work continually to be strong stewards of the gifts entrusted to us. A church lacking that educational platform will cease to be relevant for the future. I graduated from VTS in 1969. Today, thanks to the leadership of former dean Martha Horne, Ed Hall, Dean Ian Markham, and Barney Hawkins, a strong commitment to preserving our fragile island home is part of the character, ethos, and curriculum of the Seminary. I am proud to be a small part of the ongoing VTS environmental initiative.

19 April 1985

OK—no gifts. But how can one give nothing to two who give so much—in deed and by their very being, the way they are—"for others." A wish then, or half-wish-half-prayer!

May your union, ever old and every moment ever new, be as the bright shadow of that union that surpasses every good. May your joy reflect—and find its life and being and notion in—that joy that knows no joy beyond or beside it. And may you each in your gift to the other, shadow forth, however faintly, the gift of gifts that is yours now in our common hope, that we count upon to be ours forever in very surety.

J.R.S.

To be blessed with loving parents and grandparents is a huge advantage, and then to discover in midlife a mentor whose gifts are beyond measure is a joyous affirmation that life offers unexpected rewards. After St. Matthew's sanctuary burned to the ground, Dr. John R. Seeley showed up one-half hour early for services in our school's gymnasium, which was serving as our temporary worship space. After the service, we agreed to have lunch—and did so on a regular basis for the next thirty years. John became a guide, beacon, critic, and loving friend. He was three decades my senior and a century wiser, as indicated by this lovely "half-wish-half-prayer" he wrote to Katy and me a week before our marriage.

Small of stature, he was a giant among thinkers of the twentieth century with the gifts of discernment, wisdom, and patience. In addition to his eloquence, he shaped policy and practice on an international scale. He helped establish the Peace Corps with Sargent Shriver and was deeply invested in social justice issues. He was, above all, a devoted humble Christian who exemplified concern for justice and peace in the world throughout his ninety-five years. My family was indeed blessed to have known him.

A Creedal Declaration   1995

We believe in one God, Creator of land and sea and sky...through Him all things were made, and from Him and in Him alone they have their being...wherever there is life, He is its sole sustainer, and all forms of life on Earth derive from Him their form and function.

We believe, therefore, in the sanctity of life and the inherent and immeasurable value of each and all his creatures.

We thus revere the creation in all its richness and diversity, and all of God's wondrous Kingdoms on Earth where every form is given its appointed niche and home.

We recognize the interdependence of the human family, and the families of animals, plants, and all that are, and we value accordingly the privilege and duty of mutual subsistence.

We believe in the God of history, who reveals Himself in time and who thus sanctifies and redeems all in his Holy Creation.

Fondly, John

John was my mentor for most of my career. During our weekly lunches, we dissected, discussed, and debated issues for hours. There is no question in my mind that John was the single most influential guide and confidant—outside of my family members—in my life. Although he died in 2005, I continue to draw upon his wisdom and counsel to this day.

One day we were talking about creeds—not a common discussion even among priests, I would imagine—and sometime later this letter from John was faxed to my office. We went on to revise this declaration for over a year, and today The Seeley-Kreitler Environmental Creedal Declaration is one of the offerings from my career in which I take great pride. The creed went through six revisions and the finished product was debuted May 5, 1996 at St. Matthew's. Eleven years later, at the April 27, 2007 Water of Life Conference at Virginia Theological Seminary, seminarians and clergy had an opportunity to recite the creed as well.

This writing partnership was symbolic of our long-term relationship and part of the incredible legacy he left to his beloved Episcopal Church, to me, and my family—especially to our daughter Laura—and to countless others. Thanks John! You will never be forgotten.

Dear Peter, *5/12/85*

You always like a good little story, often have a chance to repeat it, and often do (to the listener's delight).

Mother's Day brought me Alec Guinness's new [book] Blessings in Disguise*. The "blessings" Sir Alec counts are characteristically the people who have affected his life, Ralph Richardson for one.*

Guinness was never certain precisely what Richardson believed in, except motorcycles and gin, until on one occasion he rose to his feet, stood at attention, and raised his beaker in a military-style toast, "To Jesus Christ. What a splendid chap!"

Cheers,

Love,

Bink

A clergy person does not pick his or her parishioners, and personalities of all types cross our thresholds on a weekly basis. Bink was just one of those wonderful characters. Like other lay volunteers, Bink was a great asset to the church. She served on our altar guild, which, in The Episcopal Church, prepares all the accoutrements necessary for performing our sacerdotal functions.

Bink was a true Anglophile and loved everything British and, most especially, all things royal. She had a great sense of humor and a style that was immediately evident. She was known for her hats and, like the Queen, it seemed she changed them daily. I saw her often because of her service to the church and I listened to many of her stories and, as she admits, often repeated them.

As my dad reminded me, be extra kind to those who serve you. Yes, be respectful of the volunteers in the parish—indeed, all those who help us.

I raise my glass to Bink. What a splendid dame!

Peter,

I think Christianity is an eventide melancholy religion. I prefer the morning philosophy, bright with promise and expectation—anticipation of good things rather than melancholy and sad events [that] cannot be altered. This may account for some of the differences in the way we interpret our respective concepts of religion.

Peter

It is such a shame that this letter didn't include a last name or an address because I think the two of us Peters could have benefited from an ongoing dialogue. It has always been gratifying to me to receive letters like this one. I value that aspect of another's humanity that questions religion; even the most spiritual or religious among us have doubts or questions along our journey. Wrestling with one's faith is as ancient as human history, and in my case that process never seems to end. Chances are that we will encounter many people in life who see the glass as half empty rather than as half full, although my guess is that more of us prefer to associate with people who anticipate good things. If Christianity has become a melancholy religion in the eyes of some, we priests need to take that perception seriously. If we were paying attention in seminary, we came away preaching a religion of springtime, hope, and resurrection. Sadness is a natural part of the human experience, yet a personal spiritual foundation, anchored in the promise and expectation of each new day, can sustain us through the hard times.

March 20, 1987

Pastor Pete:

Back in the '60s I attended a prayer meeting in Pasadena under the Episcopal banner. That night we prayed for Bishop Pike, then, in the midst of the service, Episcopal brothers and sisters began to sing in tongues—the most beautiful harmony imaginable.

I am writing to you because someone came to spy on me shortly after I had written that blistering letter to you. I went out in the rain to see about my own car. Then I noticed someone in a car behind mine and that person started her engine as I came up. Who was that?

Sincerely,

Roger

P.S. I appreciate your reply to my letter. We'll have to pray for one another.

My nickname as a young baseball Little Leaguer in Millburn, New Jersey was "Pistol Pete." I smiled at the manner in which Roger addressed me—I had gained another alliterative nickname—yet I was confused by his not-so-veiled implication that I had planted a spy in response to the "blistering" letter that he sent me. I have known other clergy members who have been threatened because of a political stance or a perceived radical sermon, but this letter is somewhat of a head-scratcher.

Some people have strong emotions about certain issues and can be prone to castigate others—even their pastor, rabbi, priest, or minister—simply for bringing a subject to the light of day. Thankfully, the extent of protests directed at me were limited to a handful of walk-outs during sermons or talks, plus dozens of angry letters or "nastygrams." It has been my custom to try to respond with kindness to letters of anger or threat of any kind, although I must admit that I have not always been gentle. I prefer to discuss controversial subjects face-to-face in order to have the opportunity to address an issue in depth. Letter writing is not a substitute for being present with parishioners, but sometimes it is the best we can do.

Dear Rev. Kreitler   *3/18/87*

It has been a long time since I have read anything as marvelous as this writing.

[Your article] alerted decent Americans who wish to preserve their true religious faiths and that embrace a tolerance of others' beliefs or even nonbeliefs.

We have had enough of these TV clergy who tell us we are doomed unless we accept their beliefs and also pay for it.

I trust that you will forever continue to write and speak against TV preachers' intolerance.

Very truly yours,

Max Maron

Mr. Maron's response to my *Los Angeles Times* editorial balanced out several critics of the article who derided me for being intolerant of those who preach intolerance. I am keenly aware of the power that the media can have over hearts and minds, especially of the marginalized, vulnerable, and elderly. Free speech is guaranteed—and that applies to evangelists on the airways, pundits on the radio, or bloggers on the internet—but blatant discrimination, racism, elitism, or bigotry must be called out and labeled for what it is: un-American and un-Christian. In the past, I was bold enough to write that the self-described Moral Majority was neither; now I can say the same thing about the self-labeled Religious Right.

Today there are blatantly disingenuous clergy aligning themselves with almost antichrist-like figures. Senator Daniel Webster of Massachusetts, in an address to Congress, stated, "If we are to be representatives of the people we must stand on the watchtower of liberty." This prescient statement must be applied to the clergy of today. Standing up for liberty and justice, as well as speaking truth to power, is our moral obligation as men and women of faith. Thank you, Mr. Maron, for supporting those who speak against intolerance in any form.

March 14

Dear Pete,

I was thrilled to receive the copy of your book [about the Flatiron Building], thank you so much. It is really beautiful, much more than I could have imagined. You're certainly to be congratulated.

Betsy and I spent a few days at Ocean Reef and had an especially enjoyable evening with your mother and father. I don't get to see them so much anymore. If you get out to the Cape this summer, I hope we can all get together.

Thank you again, Pete, and the best of luck in all future endeavors.

With best regards,

Love,

Aunt Tommy

I share this note from my godmother, Aunt Tommy Smith Nordblom, for a variety of reasons. Aunt Tommy was my mother's roommate at Wheaton College. She and her husband became close friends of my parents, and after her husband, Uncle Bob, died, Tommy married our neighbor and good friend, Robert Nordblom of Harwich Port, Cape Cod.

Aunt Tommy was a wonderful role model as I was growing up. I have always viewed godparents as additional on-call adult guarantors. During the baptism, the priest asks, "Will you be responsible for seeing that the child you present is brought up in the Christian faith and life?" We know today that "it takes a village to raise a child" and that having other adults to co-parent children is prudent in these challenging times. Every community of faith should place a stronger emphasis on the rite of baptism and the role of godparents in nurturing and guiding young people.

Dear Father Peter,   *2/6/91*

I can't believe that you're really leaving. Just because you are leaving doesn't mean that the memory of all your chapels will be gone. As an individual, I know that I will never forget you, but I know I share this feeling with many others. I remember that rainy Easter day that you baptized me. I want to wish you good luck with your new job.

Sincerely,

Jennifer (age 12)

P.S. When I get older, I want you to marry me!

I was privileged to know many of our children's friends; Jennifer was in our daughter Laura's class. Working with young people affords a clergy person surprises beyond measure. Rambunctious, self-absorbed, focused on popularity, addicted to social media, and yet still so utterly wonderful, children—especially teenagers—can keep us on our toes and young at heart. And while it's pretty easy to tell from their body language and other signs whether or not you are getting through to young people, a letter from a twelve-year-old speaks volumes. The fact that Jennifer recalled "that rainy Easter day that you baptized me" is special. A businessman friend from Atlanta by the name of Jim Jacoby once said to me that after success comes significance. When working with young people, significance often comes before success; yet when a letter like Jennifer's comes across your desk maybe there is also some success after all.

Invest your gifts and talents in young people, even for just a couple of years, during the course of your ministry. The time you share with a younger person will leave a lasting and treasured imprint on you both.

2-10-91

Dear Peter,

I am very sorry to hear about your departure, but I agree with your profession for the future. I will miss your gems of wisdom on Sunday [mornings], i.e., "It is not what you do on Sunday, but what you do on the days between Sundays that count[s]."

Take care—our prayers are with you and your family.

    Affectionately,

    Jean E. + "3"

Jean lost her husband, Hal, at an early age and has been as faithful a Sunday worshipper as I have ever known. The number "3" in quotation marks in her signature block refers to her wonderful children whom she essentially raised on her own. This simple note of affirmation regarding my decision to leave the parish church and work on environmental issues was the kind of encouragement that made the hard decision easier.

I also appreciated Jean's reference to one of my sermons. In my experience, it is rare to receive a direct quote from a sermon that touched someone so directly. It cannot be emphasized enough that since we ascend the pulpit every Sunday without knowing every detail of every parishioner's life, we can't understand fully what our words may mean to each of them. Our word, as the Toltec people of Mesoamerica wrote, should be impeccable; at a minimum, we must always try to have our word match our behavior.

Dear Peter,

Holly, Fraser, and I continue to be overwhelmed by the depth of love and support that has come our way since Chuck died. It has been remarkable and we are all deeply grateful. It was lovely of you to write...[Y]our generous and reassuring words have meant more than you can know. Please accept, in return of your thoughtfulness, the gratitude of the entire family. God's grace and peace to you. May He continue to hold all of us under the shadow of his wings.

Fondly, Lydia

Dear Peter,

Your note was lovely and the photos priceless. Thanks so very much for sending them. I worship in that space[30] often and it feels wonderful to see him in the photos standing there. He was a wonderful reader, wasn't he? I thought so too. Thanks for telling me. I hear from Carol that you've had your fight with an evil disease yourself and that you're winning. Good for you and good for all of us that you are. We are survivors it seems. My warmest best wishes and gratitude. I hope we see each other again...soon again.

Love, Lydia

I have included two letters from Mrs. Charlton Heston—Lydia—a lady for whom I had the greatest respect. Mrs. Heston was one of the most gracious, humble, and talented women I have ever met. Her notes illuminate the character of a great person. The reassurance in the second note and her insightful comment, "We are survivors it seems" reflect a depth of caring and an honest admission that we all have challenges in life. Lydia's words resonate and embolden me to this day, as have those of so many other older people whom I've had the pleasure of knowing. I love the poetic last line of her first note. Whether one is overtly religious or spiritual or not, being held "under the shadow of his wings" speaks to the feeling of being comforted and protected by someone who always cares about us. It is a blessing to perceive that someone—be it God, a family member, or a friend—holds us under their wings.

Lydia and I shared a love of photography. My family was particularly fond of her photos of religious iconography from around the world that she incorporated into her famous Christmas cards. Finding common ground with a wide range of friends, family members, coworkers, or parishioners has greatly enriched my life and ministry.

---

[30]St. Matthew's.

The church is being challenged at this moment in history to rearticulate its understanding and purpose for all of God's creation. We cannot ignore this challenge.

> The Right Reverend Edmund Browning, 24th Presiding Bishop of The Episcopal Church

July 10, 1990

Dear Peter,

Today I am asking you to be a participant in a consultation [that] I am convening in order to prepare a major policy resolution on the environment and sustainable development for the General Convention.

This is a crucial moment for the world, a time that I believe we need to seek common security for all nations, with particular attention to the environmental crisis and the economic and social systems that drive it.

The church is being challenged at this moment in history to rearticulate its understanding and purpose for all of God's creation. We cannot ignore this challenge.

I believe this gathering holds the promise for our Church to move to a leadership role in addressing the global crisis we now face. I cannot think of a meeting that I have summoned which has been faced with a more serious task.

Edmund L. Browning

Presiding Bishop

Clergy receive a plethora (sorry, but this is one of my favorite words) of invitations throughout their careers, but this one stood out for me and forever shaped my career and theology.

Presiding Bishop Browning was the "big boss" of The Protestant Episcopal Church in the United States of America, better known as The Episcopal Church. His prophetic words thirty years ago—"I believe this gathering holds the promise for our Church to move to a leadership role in addressing the global crisis we now face. I cannot think of a meeting that I have summoned which has been faced with a more serious task"—did not fall on deaf ears.

If only more Christian leaders would stop excusing political leaders who, because of their choices and votes, are imperiling God's gift of creation. My eternal gratitude to Bishop Browning for his vision and leadership.

> June 2
>
> Ahoy Peter!
> What a wonderful craft you have fashioned! Oh just so terrific! I can't find the words! And Katie when you hang up the lacy curtains you're making inside it will be able to glide into the sea. Now I'm off to buy a bottle of champagne to crash on the bow!
> All hands on deck!!
> Jeanne

About five years ago, I started collecting the wine corks that friends, family and The Bel-Air Bay club were discarding. I didn't know at the time what I would do with the corks, but I did not want them to end up in a landfill. Eventually I decided to build an ark using my corks. I hired a boat builder to create a twelve and one-half foot, double-ended fiberglass hull. I then spent seven months covering it by hand with approximately twelve thousand corks—primarily from wine bottles, with a few hundred champagne and tequila corks for variety.

I displayed the finished ark in several venues: an art gallery, at the fiftieth anniversary celebration of the Marina del Rey, and at the Bel-Air Bay Club. The ark served as more than a fun display of repurposing and recycling. With the ark as my backdrop, I retold the story of the first great flood and added the warning that we could experience another catastrophic sea-level rise in the future. I purposely coupled the biblical story of Noah with the danger of climate change and its role in the accelerating degradation of God's creation. I called the craft *Adam's Ark*, because it represents hope for all of humanity.

Jeanne's delightful response to *Adam's Ark* and to my lecture reinforced my belief in the teaching value of historical stories. Jeanne, another of my elder friends, is a gem of a lady with a wonderful attitude about life. Katy and I visit with her regularly. She and her late husband, Wilson, remain role models for us as they both aged gracefully and with dignity.

St. Benedict's Monastery

Cistercian Monks

Dear Peter,

Here, at last, is the stole you commissioned for Earth Day. The fabric is completely natural (wool on a cotton warp) and the colors are true earth tones like hickory, bramble, sagebrush, lichen etc. Hope you really like it.

It is hard coming up with something when I haven't seen the environment where it's going to be used, but I trust it will work for you. I really enjoyed doing it and appreciate very much the freedom you gave me for color and design. I will be anxious to know how you like it.

A blessed Easter to you and your family.

In Peace,

Rick Bowers

One of the great blessings of The Episcopal Church is that priests are encouraged to take a sabbatical—time off for study, reflection, exploration, and action. Part of my 1990 exploration was spent at St. Benedict's Monastery in Snowmass, Colorado. Eating meals in silence, worshipping twice a day, participating in guided meditations, and taking walks in the middle of winter on ten thousand snow-covered acres was a treat. I met Rick at St. Benedict's. He had a loom on which he wove the most beautiful handcrafted stoles. A stole is the large ribbon a priest wears around his or her neck and is the one gift given at ordination that represents the priesthood. I have several special ones that I have acquired, such as a macramé stole woven by a Native American descendent, a colorful stole from Mexico, and the one of natural fibers and colors from St. Benedict's. I treasure all three; each is an outward and visible sign of an inward and spiritual grace. The symbolism of a stole is similar to that of a wedding ring because, to me, a stole represents loyalty, dedication, and commitment.

Loomis Chaffee School

Dear Peter,

I wanted to thank you once again for the terrific way in which you led the memorial service for alumni. It was a fitting and lovely way to remember the many Loomis Chaffee people who passed away this year.

Your talk was particularly memorable and moving and I hope you will submit a copy to the magazine.

    Best wishes,

        Sheila

At the conclusion of my junior year at the Loomis School, the chaplain, Rev. Carl Munger, approached me and asked if I would consider being the student chaplain for my senior year. "Why me?" I inquired." Because I think you would do a good job," he responded. I remember smiling inwardly because I had been asked to serve as head of the dance committee as well.

Pay attention when a respected elder taps you on your shoulder during your "absorbing" years. The chaplain saw something in me that took me many years to discover for myself. To this day I acknowledge with deep appreciation the teachers from my formative years. For me to return to my prep school for our fiftieth reunion and lead the memorial service was an honor. My sermon was titled "The Top Ten Lessons I Learned at Loomis," one of which was to use creativity in my sermons, talks, and chapel lessons. I even had the opportunity to thank history teacher Al Beebe, who was present for my talk. My admiration for the leadership of former headmasters Francis Grubbs and John Ratte and current Head of School and President Sheila Culbert continues to grow. We used to state "Loomis: Builder and Mother of Men"—now women and men. Loomis certainly helped me define who I am today and all who attend the school today are blessed to be attending such a fine institution.

Dear Reverend Kreitler,

Thank you for your nice letter regarding my correspondence with President Reagan. Or did you know it was a correspondence? You referred only to a letter I wrote to him. Just in case you might not be aware that my first letter resulted in a real exchange, I am enclosing a set of our letters.

We much appreciate your offer to help, and sometime very soon we will be in touch. Martin Marty, by the way, was a very early member of our advisory board, and in the years since has become a close personal friend. I think of him as having the best mind in America. It was good of you to send me his article and I want to thank you for that too.

    Sincerely,

    Norman Lear

There is an old familiar saying, "If you want to get the job, done ask a busy person." It has been my experience that writing a letter with a sincere request, suggestion, or even criticism, to a person like Mr. Norman Lear often yields a thoughtful response in return. Mr. Lear personifies a truth about many people who have contributed to the overall good of society; they pay homage to mentors who have gifts and talents for which they are grateful. Mr. Lear invited me to his home and we discussed the important role that mentorship plays in all professions. Religious historian Martin Marty would most likely have returned the accolade to Mr. Lear. As creator and producer of some of America's most beloved and iconic television shows, Mr. Lear shed light on issues like racism and bigotry that are complex and perplexing to us all.

This busy man who made time for a stranger touched my heart. A lesson learned: do not feel intimidated by the rich and powerful, for often they have achieved their success by being good listeners. A thoughtful, well-crafted letter has great power in and of itself and may shift the thinking of even the most intransient person.

Dear Peter,

Once again, my heartfelt thanks to you for all your love and support to our family in the time surrounding Wade's death. Your sensitivity and words at the service and interment brought great comfort to all of us. Your gift of friendship is something I will always treasure.

Wade's sister who lives in Northern California was not able to travel to the service. We are preparing a package to send her some of the many items people shared with us. Would you by any chance have a copy of your homily? If so, would you care to let us include it?

Thank you again, Peter, for everything you are and everything you do.

Love,

Kathy

Perhaps I am a maverick when it comes to the use of the Bible, the Book of Common Prayer, and the Episcopal marriage service, but I have always tried to approach each as casuistic and not apodictic. I view each of these texts as important road maps, but believe we can use them to chart different routes. Each time a sacramental function is performed, it should be approached on a case-by-case basis. Each child of God is unique and special in my eyes, so I have always tried to make each baptismal, marital, or burial service personal in some fashion.

The last part of Kathy's note underscores the importance of clergy keeping notes and copies of sermons, talks, or homilies (short sermons). Without copies, we can be misquoted or find ourselves unable to help those people, such as Kathy's sister-in-law, who were not able to attend the service. And as I hope that *Dear Father Peter* has demonstrated, letters also possess long-term value and should also be archived.

Dear Peter,

Please don't take my feelings as representing anyone else's because I have not discussed this with anyone else.

To me, a full life is doing your job, as you see fit—which, in my present circumstances, is practicing medicine; trying to be as good a father and husband as I can be, which I usually do not do, but I try; and also doing what I can in the social issues and socio-economic parts of our community...

I would be happy to talk to you about this sometime, but the most important thing, I hope, is that our discussions can be on the basis of mutual respect, and sometimes our actions and relations at the vestry meeting do not reflect this.

I am sending you this without revision and hope you can understand.

    Blaine Hibbard Rx

Dr. Blaine Hibbard was the chief of staff at St. Luke's Hospital in Kansas City, Missouri, an early advocate of mine, and one of the most influential lay people in my career.

In 1970 he stood up to my bishop, who had been hesitant to accept me into his diocese. Due in part to Blaine's intervention, I was admitted and ordained on April 27, 1970. A couple years later, I arrived—with hair down to my shoulders and a motorcycle helmet under my arm—to visit a teenaged parishioner who had overdosed and been admitted to St. Luke's Hospital under arrest. The diligent staffers took one look at me and, not believing that I was a priest, denied me access. Luckily, Blaine overrode them and authorized my visits.

Blaine confided in me that he felt pressured to give more of his time and talent to the church than he could reasonably give; I understood fully. He stated his priorities as his family, his profession, and his community, including his church. (Amen, my friend.) Perhaps we, the leaders of communities of faith—or businesses for that matter—ask too much of some laity, especially those who are in demanding professions and are raising a family. Blaine helped me to understand more fully one of the aspects of church life that is tricky for many people: the need to set reasonable expectations and to respect one another's boundaries.

Dear Father Peter,

How I like the week.

1. *Monday Oct. 12, 1981.....Good*
2. *Tuesday Oct. 13, 1981.....Boaring [sic]*[31]
3. *Wednesdad [sic] Oct. 14, 1981.....Good*
4. *Thursday Oct. 15, 1981.....Bad*
5. *Friday Oct. 16, 1981.....Good*
6. *Saturday Oct. 17, 1981.....Bad*
7. *Sunday Morning Oct. 18, 1981.....Good*

Love, Sarah

I really enjoyed making it fun for the students in St. Matthew's chapel programs to develop an understanding of biblical history. They were more likely to learn historical facts and do their homework when we coupled their studies with the popular game of Bible Baseball. One time I asked the students to reflect upon the past week at school and then to write me a note describing that week. This was my favorite letter describing how the week went. It was a succinct, honest reflection of what had basically been a good week for young Sarah. Kids do say the "darndest things."

Experiential chapel was the key as I strove to make the dry words in ancient books come alive for young people. The engaging films from Paulist Productions and Father Bud Kaiser were especially effective. Slides that I had taken of village life in Mexico in 1965 and India in 1963 helped the students to relate to the lives of others in places, cultures, and circumstances far removed from their world. One of my favorite chapel assignments was to have the young people draw some aspect of the Christmas narrative. I then copied the pictures to slides, arranged them in chronological order, and did a slide show during the family service on Christmas Eve. For many other Christmas Eve services, I dressed up as Bishop Nicholas of Myra. I was made up by Hollywood make-up artist Dana Nye and wore an ornate cope given to me by Bishop Robert Rusack. Another time I memorized and recited Dr. Seuss' *How the Grinch Stole Christmas* at the ever-popular family service. Making the stories relevant and interesting was my job and I took it seriously. To this day, I still believe in the power of creativity, fun, and games like Bible Baseball to engage children and to imprint lessons and important concepts on their young minds.

---

[31] I have transcribed the source letter as written in order to present it authentically.

Bradford, my oldest child, lives in Carmel, California and is a dedicated chef and single parent of Belle, our eldest granddaughter. Brad has never been known for communicating on a regular basis—he's more comfortable writing recipes than letters—but, to my delight, a surprise note or card does arrive occasionally.

This Father's Day card—leave it to a chef to find a card that features a kitchen accident—was an overt nod to his feelings about the past "OOPS!" episodes in his life. All of us parents can relate to our kids making mistakes, but we all find encouragement when a child expressly states that "things will get brighter." For me, the essence of religion is to love your God and your fellow humans through both the ups and the downs of life. Give the grace of another chance to the people you care about and love.

When I think back on those Spaceballs *shooting days at your beautiful church, I'm flooded with happy memories.*
  Mel Brooks

> Just a quick note to thank you once again for everything. My wife and I enjoyed the bottle of wine from you and your wife very much.
>
> All the best
> Mel Brooks

The opening and closing wedding scenes of the Hollywood movie *Spaceballs*, produced and directed by Mel Brooks, was filmed in St. Matthew's sanctuary. Rick Moranis, Bill Pullman, and the late John Candy were three of the actors in this parody of *Star Wars*. I was curious about the process of filmmaking and was given permission to join the set on a daily basis. I was even able to photograph when the cameras were not rolling. It was a unique and enjoyable experience, especially sitting next to Mr. Brooks as we viewed the dailies from our director chairs. I share this story to offer a life lesson that my interactions with Mr. Brooks reinforced: do not make assumptions about others, not even Hollywood celebrities. We are all capable of prejudgment, but once again my preconceived ideas were wrong. Mr. Brooks, cast, and crew were polite, respectful of our property, and a joy to be around during the entire three weeks of filming, even though the description of movie making—hurry up and then wait—was spot on. His thank-you note and the note that he sent along with his release form for this book cement my appreciation for the content of Mr. Brooks' character. He is a man who has brought joy to millions for generations and continues to do so, even as he gets closer and closer to being the "2000-year-old man" he portrayed in 1961. Amen!

> **MEL BROOKS**
>
> March 5, 2019
>
> Dear Father Peter,
>
> When I think back on those SPACEBALLS shooting days at your beautiful church I'm flooded with happy memories. I'm so pleased to be included in your new book.
>
> All the best,
> Mel Brooks

My late cousin, Richard "Dick" Kreitler, wrote me a two-word letter wishing me the best as I began my environmental ministry. Frankly, "Uncle Dick's"[32] letter of only twenty-three characters looks like a modern-day tweet. Today Twitter, Instagram, and Facebook dominate communications, and I am technologically batting 0 for 3. Dick, on the other hand, was an early adopter of email back in the mid-1990s and was a prolific email correspondent to the very end of his life. He often used digital media to share his political and social positions. His adopted means of communication was an early indicator to me that digital proficiency would become another skill set that would be required of seminarians, priests, and even bishops. Part of any clergy person's career is defined by how he or she writes—whether it is a letter, a sermon, a newsletter, or a social media post. Perhaps every seminary would be well served to offer a course on modern day methods of correspondence.

The old maxim about unintended consequences applies here, however. Today, texting or tweeting have all but replaced letters as the preferred vehicle of expression for the younger generations. I became aware of this phenomenon when my teenaged grandchildren, Megan, Belle, and Theo, began communicating with me via these channels. Granted, human dialogue has progressed from the Ten Commandments etched in stone to words typed on a computer and tucked in the cloud for perpetuity, but I cast my vote for the hand-crafted note—such as this one, which means a great deal to me.

---

[32] When we both became parents, we gave each other honorific nicknames. I called him "Uncle Dick" and he called me "Uncle Pete."

Sunday Nov. 4, 1984

Thank you, Dear Peter

Trudy Cushing

I do not recall what prompted this brief note of thanks, but this single lady with a special twinkle, Trudy Cushing, was well into her eighties when I first met her. She lived in a condemned property on the beach, built on the sands of Santa Monica Bay at the borderline of Pacific Palisades and Malibu, California. She lived alone, was personally like an ancient cypress tree—tan, gnarled, weathered—and was generous of spirit. When her home was taken by a storm and she had no place to live, she moved, as I vaguely recall, back to her loving family someplace. Whenever I drive by that small empty stretch of beach, I think of my friend.

The remarkable Archbishop Emeritus of Cape Town Desmond Tutu declared at a memorable clergy conference in the Diocese of Los Angeles during the mid-1970s, **"the divine spark is in everyone; it is our job [as priests] to help them discover that for themselves."** Trudy, wherever you may be, I offer with heartfelt appreciation a warm hug of thanks for making Bishop Tutu's prescient words come alive for me. You had a spark; your love of life, especially the sea around you and your church community of faith, was infectious. You never sought much in the way of material possessions, but your life was rich and you enriched others in your presence.

I agree 100 percent with the voice of the people of South Africa, Desmond Tutu. There is a spark in everyone; granted, it is oftentimes really hard to find, but it is there.

Sunday Nov. 4, 2018

Thank you, Dear Trudy

Father Peter

Perhaps the best way to describe our multifaceted and unpredictable role as clerics is simply to echo the words of this youngster, "You have dun a lot for me."

Rarely do we fully understand the impact we have on others as we practice our ministry. The simplest gestures of support, or a brief visit at an opportune time, or a well-crafted sermon may have long-term beneficial effects. And yet, we usually don't know unless we are told. It has been my experience that adults are more effusive in their praise, quicker in their condemnation, and more accustomed to writing a note or letter than are young people. However, when a letter does arrive from one of the youngest among us—even if it is addressed to someone named "petter"[33]—the smile of appreciation is the widest. When someone tells you that you "have made the sunny said (side) come up," you have done your job. We all face times of darkness during our lives. Given that the concept of resurrection and new beginnings is integral to our theology, the simple concept of "the sunny side of life" is something that all ages can understand. In fact, it would be a great sermon topic.

---

[33]I'm also going to assume that Kimberly didn't want me to *leave*, rather than didn't want me to *live*.

Dear Father Kreitler,   *4/11/97*

I am one of Uncle Norman's nieces who attended his memorial service last Wednesday, and I wanted to tell you again (I said on my way out, in the midst of confusion and many people, "You are rare.") how very special it was to attend that service. This is not only because of family connections. Honestly, I could not believe the words I was hearing from you! I have just about abandoned hope for the traditional church to take a leadership role in shifting consciousness, in modeling new ways of thinking for our planet. I have been a great supporter of Matthew Fox and Creation Spirituality, but have pretty much left the church behind as an immovable bastion of the old patriarchal world. So, when I heard ideas during the service like diversity, equity, corporate responsibility, earth stewardship, matriarchy, and recognition of Native American traditions, wisdom keepers, oral traditions, I was dumbfounded, shocked, ecstatic. It was so wonderfully expansive and hopeful! I love how you spoke of the Hebrew tradition of sitting around the fire telling stories and how you invited the congregation to join in the Lord's Prayer, "if it was our custom." I simply can't tell you how thrilling this was to hear. How respectful. How open-minded. How full of justice and responsibility. I wish you could be Pope!

I don't know where your parish is, and I hope this letter will find you. If you were in my neck of the woods (which is wilderness country in Northern New Mexico) I would be sitting in the front row on a regular basis. As it is, I'm happy where I am, and I hope your following grows one hundredfold and greater, and that your news may be heard by great numbers of people. It was worth coming out of the wilderness and enduring a day of travel to hear you and know there may be hope for the church after all. It was a great gift to me.

    Sincerely,

        Virginia Mudd

Priests should make it a priority to make room for teachable moments during communion, baptism, weddings, funerals, and memorial services. Making the sacraments special and unique, rather than rote recitations from stale prayer books, might be the practice of the future church. This unexpected and thoughtfully crafted letter helped me realize more than twenty years ago that I wanted my preaching to stay true to the messages of inclusivity and partnership that I learned early on in my life. Sometimes it takes a letter that "pats you on the back" to keep going. Every single person participating in the sacerdotal functions of a community of faith deserves to be treated as special. The creativity and effort that we clerics invest in making the sacraments personal and relatable honors the fact that no two people are alike. Thank you, Virginia, for your lovely letter acknowledging my attempt and for appreciating my vision of what religion should be today.

Dear Fr. Kreitler,   *January 2019*

I hope you have had a wonderful holiday season. I just finished my first semester at college. I know I will learn a lot here.

The forest that surrounds my school is great for hikes and simply walking to class, it is very peaceful. I have a study spot with a beautiful view of the ocean and open fields. The natural feeling of the campus really breathes tranquility in my life. I know I can make it through these next few years. They may be difficult, but I have friends who will help me out, both for class and with whatever personal issues I may be dealing with.

And like my grandfather, I will always do my best to help and care for them and others around me and will persevere through hardships with my willpower to overcome. Thank you for everything that you have done to help me get here. I truly appreciate you keeping me in your prayers. I wish you the best in the upcoming year.

From,

Jarrod Garcia-Guzman

Jarrod's grandfather Manuel was the sexton, caretaker, and all-around-do-everything guy at St. Matthew's Parish for over thirty-five years. He was also a humble, caring immigrant who came from a rural village in Mexico with his lovely wife, Edmunda, and who had an impact on the lives of many. In the Episcopal tradition we designate certain persons as perpetual deacons or servants of God; Manuel deserved that accolade. He was a man who never wavered in his service to the church and he became a good friend. I started calling him *el guapo*, Spanish for "the handsome one," and he would laugh and return the favor.

His daughter Velma and her two children grew up at St. Matthew's. They also smiled at my fractured Spanish and, like Manuel, would correct the grammar that I never mastered. Any support we give Edmunda and Manuel is an easy thank-you for the many years of support and help from them. I've been blessed to live and work with a variety of individuals from God's rainbow of humanity. I count the Guzman family as one of those blessings.

Peter,

I am probably being a hypocrite, and narrow, but so many of the parishioners and vestry have shown such sincere concern. Perhaps there is a mail mix-up, but it is well that I take tranquilizers when the rector hasn't even sent a two-sentence note saying he hoped I was recovering. My patience is always a bit too short—but at the moment I am pissed off...

Any glossing over it now wouldn't work—the sooner the change the better—and I don't give a damn if you quote me or not.

Hey guru...You're OK. Sometimes, that is?

This undated, unsigned letter highlights one of the many challenges of being a priest, minister, or rabbi serving a congregation. I have no idea who crafted this note or when it was sent. Anonymity was the chosen signature of many letters that I received during my career.

When the rector, the person often seen as the representative of God, fails to acknowledge something that a parishioner feels should be acknowledged, that leader is perceived as being derelict in his or her duties. I assume by the salutation at the end of the note that I was OK most of the time, which is some consolation, and that his anger was directed at my boss. Regardless of who had provoked his ire, I took the message to heart.

I have always honored speaking truth to power in any institution, including a congregation, as a method of holding leaders accountable. Even if the criticism is harsh or unwarranted, we are called to listen. Amen!

Dear Peter,

Hi! How are you doing? My family is doing fine. Thank you for all thing [sic]. We always remember you. I wish you a very best of all thing [sic] in life.

Peter we are inviting you and family to have a dinner here with us, looking forward to meet [sic] you again. On Saturday at 6:30 pm. If you Can or Can't make it Please call.

    Vanyon Mangkornkeo

During the late 1970s, the world became aware of the murderous dictatorship of Pol Pot in Cambodia. Pol Pot and the Khmer Rouge slaughtered roughly 1.8 million people—twenty percent of the nation—between 1975-1979. St. Matthew's decided to sponsor a family of five refugees escaping the horror. Mom, dad, and three children—Vanyon, Kimpon, and Latte—took up residence in one room of my modest home along with my wife, our two children, two dogs, a cat, and two rabbits. Vanyon's family came from a rural northern Cambodian tribe called the Lao Muong. They had never left their immediate surroundings, yet were willing to take their chances on our nation. They arrived with head lice but no cavities, thanks to their diet of rice, fish, and vegetables. They had never used a toilet, so our two-week task prior to settling them in their own apartment was to fast-track their acculturation. After about a year in Long Beach, California, the family moved to Texas. It has been a remarkable journey for them and an example to me and to others of what a church community can accomplish when it opens its loving arms to immigrants.

P.S. After a year of the American diet, everyone in Vanyon's family had cavities. The sugar in our diet has its downside.

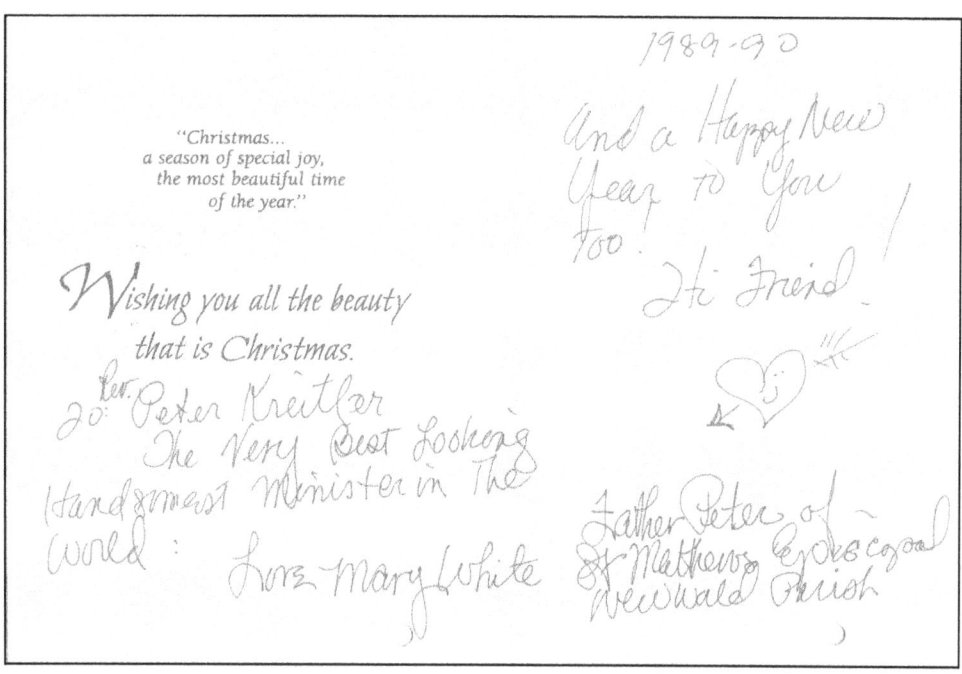

More and more people today live without a place to call home or a safe place to lay their head. One quarter of the more than five hundred thousand homeless people in our country live in California,[34] but practically every town and city wrestles with our collective responsibility to care for the least fortunate among us. Communities of faith and non-profits have led the way to find solutions.

Mary White grew up in Pacific Palisades and had been homeless for years when she arrived on the doorsteps of our parish. I had worked with other local churches to create a voucher system for those in need, but the grocery stores would only accept these promissory notes for food. Mary could not function well without her medication, so we spent a lot of time negotiating with doctors and other medical providers and with her family, who, sadly, were incapable of helping. We lost track of her years ago, but the challenge remains. New faces with similar needs inhabit our canyons and alleyways. I tried, although I'm not sure I succeeded. The words of Dr. Glenn Lopez, who treats homeless people, haunt me to this day, "It [homelessness] becomes like [living in] a third world environment." Forgetting about the least fortunate among us should never be acceptable to any of us!

---

[34]According to the U.S. Department of Housing and Urban Development, in January 2018, 129,972 of the nation's 554,000 homeless people lived in California.

Patriotism is a permanent emotion for us all. Yours is strong.
  Tom Hanks

Dear Peter Kreitler,

I had time to look at your patriotic magazine project, which is obviously a very personal passion. We all are blessed with such passions.

I have no idea what wider, popular future your idea has, but I wish you continued enjoyment. Patriotism is a permanent emotion for us all. Yours is strong.

All good things,

    Tom Hanks

One of the pillars of integrity in the Hollywood community is actor, producer, and collector of World War II memorabilia Tom Hanks. Rita Wilson and Tom's son attended St. Matthew's school and they were actively involved as parents for many years. Because of his personal support for veterans and his collection of patriotic memorabilia, I asked him to comment on my United States flag magazine project; this letter is how he responded.

My grandparents taught me to appreciate the meaning behind Old Glory. It's more than a piece of cloth attached to a stick, and I revere what the flag stands for. I have woven the themes of patriotism and the meaning of love of country into our Fourth of July worship services on many occasions. A priest has a free pulpit—with the caveat that we are encouraged to avoid partisan politics or preaching for or against an individual candidate. My love of this country is due in large part to its religious tolerance and its guarantee of freedom of speech, unless that speech constitutes a hate-filled diatribe against—or otherwise violates the legal rights of—others. Our nation's religious pluralism—the fact that we have many religions (and not a state religion) as well as the freedom not to hold religious beliefs—makes our nation strong. The fact that we are free to express our views about these beliefs makes it great.

Dear Mr. Kreitler,

It has been an inspiration to review your "labor of love." You have done a superb job. I thank you for including two excerpts from my June 14, 1975 speech at Fort Benning:

> *Whenever I see Old Glory, on whatever occasion, there is a warm reaction in my heart and mind, as the American flag stands for the finest tradition in our nation's history of two centuries plus. There is a very special excitement when I see our flag in Washington, DC flying above the Supreme Court, the U.S. Capitol, and the White House because it symbolically ties together, under our Constitution, the judicial, legislative, and executive branches of our government, which are the fundamental strengths of our governmental system.*

Regards,

Gerald R. Ford

This excerpt from President Ford's speech echoes my feelings about the flag and evokes memories of raising Old Glory that go as far back as being at my grandfather's house during the Second World War. President Ford's words remain relevant for today, especially when he speaks of the fundamental strengths of our triune and balanced governmental system. Our flag emits powerful messages of inclusivity, justice, and liberty for all. That is a strong messaging platform that our religious institutions embrace as well. I am reminded that the three congregations that I have served all displayed two flags in the sanctuary: the flag of The Episcopal Church and the flag of the United States. I have preached on the meaning behind the Stars and Stripes and have invited the Pacific Palisades Oom PA PA band to play patriotic music on the Sundays closest to the Fourth of July. I have also built a collection of over four thousand magazines, spanning the years 1839 to the present, with the United States flag on the cover. Why all this flag interest? I was raised in a nation that fosters freedom and justice for all. When I raise the flag, I am reminded of the freedoms I have been able to experience, both as a citizen of the United States of America and as a priest of the church.

P.S. President Ford graciously waived his post-presidency speaking fee when he addressed St. Matthew's School. What a treat for all of us!

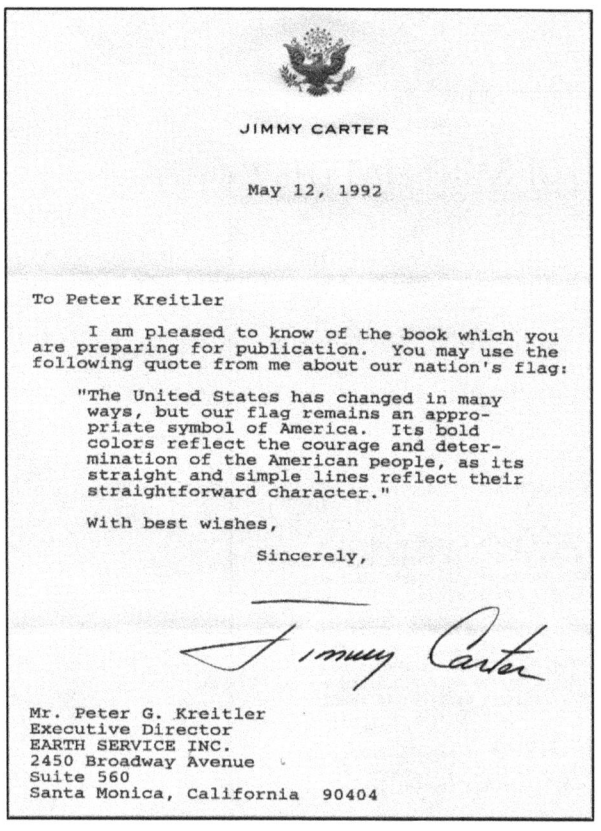

Although I have not had the pleasure of meeting President Carter, I have always admired him from afar. I treasure my signed photos of him—one of Carter with Menachem Begin and Anwar Sadat at the signing of the Camp David peace accord and one of Carter sitting for his presidential portrait with the famous photographer Yousuf Karsh.[35] I wrote President Carter about my book that features magazine covers depicting the United States flag; he wrote me this letter in response.

Jimmy Carter's post-presidency commitment to helping others has won him a higher level of respect and appreciation than he was awarded during his presidency. I have noticed that when some people reach retirement age, they not only stop going to the office, but also abdicate involvement in our national story. As of this writing, President Carter, who is well into his nineties, is still working for the common good. Similarly, one aspect of the priesthood that I have long admired is that the majority of clergy, regardless of denomination, continue to try in some fashion to make this world better—even or, perhaps, especially—in retirement. Jimmy Carter is an American patriot and a wonderful post-retirement role model for all of us.

---

[35] My VTS classmate Rev. Jo Tartt became a photography and art dealer following his career as a parish priest. He orchestrated the official White House portrait of President Carter and snapped the photo during the sitting.

THE PARISH OF SAINT MATTHEW
1031 BIENVENEDA AVENUE □ P.O. BOX 37 □ PACIFIC PALISADES, CALIFORNIA 90272 □ (213) 454-1358
THE REVEREND PETER G. KREITLER

The White House
1600 Pennsylvania Ave
Washington DC 20500

January 31, 1989

Dear President Bush:

I write in reference to your comment about 1,000 points of light!

As an Episcopal priest for twenty years I have celebrated the importance of 'light' as a symbol of hope throughout my ministry. My idea, that I share combines your creative image and people of commitment throughout our 50 states.

Would it not be possible to transform the 1,000 points of light to represent the good work of 1,000 persons of light all across our land? A Presidential Citation or recognition of persons who do good on behalf of others on a grand scale - ie. 20 per state or 1,000 a year (times 4 or 8) would touch millions of people.

If each state were to submit the names of persons representing all racial, ethnic, and social economic groups your 1,000 points of light would begin to brighten the communities of our nation in new ways.

A person who 'does good' is certainly a point of light who brings hope to others. May your Presidency bring to you and your family joy amidst the challenge and responsibility.

Sincerely,

Peter Kreitler

THE WHITE HOUSE
WASHINGTON

April 3, 1989

Dear Reverend Kreitler,

The President has sent me your letter with your thoughts on volunteerism.

One of the basic missions of the Office of National Service is to encourage "points of light" to focus national and community resources that are not primarily governmental on solving critical domestic problems. As you know, all of us have an important role to play in this effort. In fact, the President has said that "from now on in America, any definition of a successful life must include serving others...."

This office is committed to developing constructive plans to improve and build on existing programs as well as creating new initiatives to serve others.

Thank you for taking the time to write.

Sincerely,

C. Gregg Petersmeyer
Deputy Assistant to the President
Office of National Service

The Reverend Peter Kreitler
Saint Matthew Parish
1031 Bienveneda Avenue
Post Office Box 37
Pacific Palisades, California 90272

I wrote President George Herbert Walker Bush on January 31, 1989 and expanded on his concept of a thousand points of light. The third paragraph of my letter spells out my thoughts and requests. I had no great expectations that my letter would be acknowledged, much less acted upon, until a letter with THE WHITE HOUSE WASHINGTON in the upper-left-hand corner of the envelope arrived, just nine weeks later, on April 5, 1989. The opening sentence, from a deputy assistant to the president of the United States, is testimony to the effectiveness of writing to our elected officials, even though they receive a flood of mail daily:

> Dear Reverend Kreitler,
>
> The President has sent me your letter with your thoughts on volunteerism…

Then, twenty-eight weeks later, on November 7, 1989, an article appeared in *The Christian Science Monitor* entitled "A Thousand Points of Light to Shine: Congress to Create Points of Light Initiative Foundation to Manage the Program." Two weeks later, on November 23, 1989, the San Francisco Chronicle stated that

> Bush announced that the White House will begin a "Points of Light" program to single out a person or institution a day exemplifying the concept of community service. Each day the White House will recognize one individual who has successfully addressed our most dire social problems by engaging in community service.

As a friend mentioned to me, "Perhaps, Peter, your letter helped to make a thousand points of light become a reality and not just a slogan."

The old adage that "it is not what you know, but whom you know" often proves itself in special ways. One of my oldest and closest friends Tim Blake was the owner of USA Marine. A supporter of President George Herbert Walker Bush contacted Tim to see if he could bring a small but well-outfitted fishing boat to Walker Point, Maine so that the president could give it to a friend as a surprise birthday present. With a Bass Tracker aluminum boat in tow, Tim arrived at the compound, where he was greeted by the First Couple and the lucky recipient of the birthday present. Having shaken hands with the president, Tim felt his day was complete, but then President Bush invited Tim to join the group on his speedboat. During the full-throttle ride, Tim and the president discussed their mutual love of blue fishing. As they docked, Tim thanked his hosts and got ready to leave. Once again, his outing was extended when the Bushes invited him to stay and have lunch with them. Following lunch, a secret service officer entered the dining room and matter-of-factly informed the president that Mikhail Gorbachev was on the phone. Sure enough, it was the famous red phone that had rung. Gorbachev had been released from house arrest and the coup that hardliners from his own government had carried out was over. President Bush jumped up from the table, motioned to Tim to follow, and my good buddy became a witness to the historical release of a world leader.

What had started as an interesting errand had turned into a surprising afternoon enjoying the hospitality of and discovering points of intersection with our forty-first president and First Lady Barbara Bush. And the ripple effects did not end there. Shortly after his visit to Walker Point, Tim paved the way for me to write to President Bush about the book I was writing on patriotism and the United States flag. The lesson is simple: never close the door to new opportunities or relationships. You never know what other doors may open that can help you to live out your ministry.

Dear Mr. Kreitler, *8/26/91*

Thank you for sharing with me your concern for the proposed pulp facility in Apple Grove, West Virginia. Recycling is a major focus of my administration, and I appreciate the opportunity to address this issue.

I can assure you that I am completely supportive of not only recycling paper, but also using the products of recycling. I have implemented policies that call for the increased use of recycled products and will continue to support legislation encouraging, or even requiring, recycling. I also support the development of this state's abundant natural resources and believe that recycling and economic development are both important to W. Virginia's future. The permit application for this plant will undergo intense scrutiny. Before the project can become a reality, we will make certain that its wastewater treatment process is state of the art and environmentally safe. I appreciate the time you took to write.

Sincerely,

Gaston Caperton

No one is completely self-made. All of us have relied on teachers, family members, and other guides along the way to help us to be who we are today. I am no different. Dr. John Seeley and I broke bread on a regular basis for thirty years. He taught me much, led by example, and—other than my family—influenced my life as much as any other individual.

I include this letter from the thirty-first governor of West Virginia (1989-1997) for a specific reason. John always encouraged me to write personal letters to public officials to present my views on an issue. For example, he was adamantly opposed to the death penalty and wrote every governor who had inmates on death row. John believed it was more effective to convey important ideas or feelings via hand-written letters rather than by electronic media, so I took a chance and wrote Governor Caperton. While I didn't know anything about him, other than that he is a Democrat, I knew about the potential damage from paper plants or mills. Politicians receive thousands of requests and suggestions, so when I received this personally signed response, I was amazed, pleased, impressed, and best of all, filled with hope.

Dear Peter,   *5/5/93*

The nuclear power industry needs more space to dump its radioactive waste. Their idea is to dump the waste in unlined dirt trenches over a groundwater aquifer fifteen miles from the Colorado River in Ward Valley, California.

I have been active in the fight to block this proposal for the past two years. The election of President Clinton and the appointment of Interior Secretary Bruce Babbitt were encouraging, but he is now facing intense lobbying by the nuclear industry.

It will take the strength of a united grassroots campaign to stop Ward Valley. I hope we can work together to halt this plan.

Tom Hayden

Tom Hayden was one of the founders of Students for a Democratic Society and was a member of the Chicago Seven, the group that was charged with conspiracy to incite riots during the 1968 Democratic Convention.[36] His contributions—through his teaching, writing, and legislative skills—to redressing injustice won him the admiration of many, myself included.

Tom was a friend and his wife Barbara was a wonderful partner. Tom encouraged clergy, in our roles as voices for God's creation, to embrace the environmental community. He challenged me intellectually and urged me to become an activist. As a priest, I was always encouraged to keep politics out of the pulpit, and I have honored that counsel. Nonetheless, when issues arose that could affect the future of my children and grandchildren, I would align myself with those who were willing to speak up on their behalf. I agreed with Tom that the collapse of creation was accelerating at the hand of man. As a result, and at Tom's request, I testified in front of the California Legislative Committee on Endangered Species. Tom's remarks during the lunch that followed in the statehouse cafeteria were as scary as they were informative. He declared that "the dumbing of America" was going to destroy our country. In many ways, Tom's frightening prophecy has come true and it haunts me to this day.

Twenty-five years ago, Tom hoped that he and I could work together. We did, although our respective health issues kept us from collaborating at the level that we had envisioned. Tom was controversial to the end, but I will always admire the persistence with which he used his voice and legislative skills to great effect.

---

[36]Although he was initially found guilty, the conviction was overturned on appeal.

Dear Peter,

There are no words to thank you now. (They'll come later.)

Thank you for always being there for our family!

Warmly,

Marianne

In many ways, this letter reflects the twinned sorrows and great rewards experienced by clergy who see their role as pastor first.

Some background regarding this letter: I had performed Marianne and Norman's wedding on the eighteenth hole of Pebble Beach Golf Links on December 3, 1977. The venue for their wedding was spectacular, but the show-stealer was Norman playing his guitar and singing to his bride. Tragically, this special and accomplished man died while body surfing in Costa Rica. This note arrived shortly after I officiated at Norman's funeral on March 28, 2014. To honor their father, the children formed a family chorus and sang the childhood songs Norman had taught them, with son Ben accompanying them on the guitar. Too few years had separated the two sacraments, but Marianne's simple letter of thanks gave me the comfort I needed when her husband—my friend—died.

Once again, I cannot overstate the importance to a successful ministry of being present in the lives of others, especially in today's busy and often impersonal world. Simply put by Marianne, just being there is often enough.

12-17-84

Dear Father Peter,

You don't know me, but I could recognize you on the street from reading about you in the Palisadian-Post. I like to read what you write. I like the way you have handled your life.

I am a former parishioner who moved out to a faraway place. Most of the people [here] are strict fundamentalists, born-again, saved, possessed by the Holy Spirit, speaking in tongues. Do they have something I don't have? Unity Magazine *decided to give baptism and the work of the Trinity the metaphysical interpretation, which is to save people by revealing to them the presence of Christ within and to recognize Christ as creative, infinite intelligence, and the Holy Spirit as the divine power and light and passion that inspired Jesus to discover and demonstrate Christ consciousness.*

This is pretty deep for me. Right now, I am rather turned off religion, but still need something. I don't feel I have any resources to carry me about. I miss the St. Matthew's sycamores.

MT

One of the grand traditions of our community of faith is that it honors independent thought. We are not encouraged to join in lockstep with everyone else as we personally explore our faith in Christ or God. MT asks whether her new fundamentalist neighbors have something she doesn't have. My answer is that I do not believe they do, other than having the comfort of surrounding themselves with like-minded individuals. No judgment intended here, but MT represents legions of people who have left organized religion because they no longer feel at home in their childhood churches and because they find evangelical Christianity flawed.

There are many paths, and who am I—or any other individual—to judge whether a person's way is inadequate or misguided? Many of the letters that have come across my desk are from people who are searching for resources to help them get through life. Maybe MT's description of what she misses is part of all of our healing and learning processes. Humanity has been given the book of nature for one hand and the scriptures of all traditions for the other hand. The Bible, Torah, Upanishads, and Koran are not always sufficient for personal growth or understanding; the other great teacher is nature. Retreating to and spending time in God's gift of creation may give us new lenses through which to interpret scripture.

To Father Peter,

Thank you for doing a nice job for my grandmother's funeral and sevice [sic]. Right now, I am going to Oklahoma to burry [sic] her. But I think you did a nice job and I want to thank you.

    From,

    Michael

Many letters arrive filled with grammar and spelling errors, but I am not about to judge, especially when the words reflect feelings from the heart. Besides, I never did well in my college English classes, so who am I to critique another person's writing?

Oftentimes a grandparent's passing is a child's first experience with death. It has been my observation over the years that young people benefit greatly when they are included in their grandparent's funeral or service of remembrance. Coupled with age-appropriate discussions about the natural cycle of life and death, the experience can go a long way towards preparing the young to handle challenges along life's journey.

As a parish priest, I always tried to engage the children or grandchildren of the deceased by offering them an opportunity to read or say something in the service itself. I learned this bit of thoughtfulness from the Reverend Herb Cooper, who read my tribute to my paternal grandfather when I could not be there for his memorial service. I never forgot this gesture of inclusion and respect.

COUNTY OF YORK, PENNSYLVANIA

H. Stanley Rebert, District Attorney

June 3, 1997

Dear Peter,

Susan and I are celebrating our twenty-fifth anniversary this year, and she would like to renew our vows. We were married by a judge in a civil ceremony in York back in 1972 and I guess she feels the Lord's blessing on this union is needed. From my perspective, there is only one "Man of God" that is capable of performing such a miracle. I suspect, however, that the practical difficulties in accomplishing this Herculean task may be formidable. Ergo my inquiries.

July 9, 1997

Dear Peter,

I can't even get my ducks in a row on this end much less ask you to travel three thousand miles to perform an unholy ceremony. So, we're on hold. I will be in touch. Thanks for your patience and Godspeed.

Sincerely,

Stan

Years after Stan and I were at Brown University together, I was able to track down my good buddy and Kappa Sigma fraternity brother because he had written me on his letterhead stationery. One of the great joys in saving letters, especially ones as warm, funny, and personal as these, is that they provide a ready access into one's memory bank. It's even more helpful when the letters are dated. During our senior year, Stan was the Brown University football mascot, Bruno the Bear. When he injured his Achilles heel, he asked me to take his place. My most memorable game was at the Yale Bowl—a game that, unbeknownst to me at the time, my parents attended. I have gotten a lot of mileage out of telling the story of that day.

Stan was also an usher in my wedding. We had a delightful chance to catch up by phone recently. We chimed in simultaneously that aging was indeed hard. We laughed and made a pledge: if we both make it to 2022, we are going to attempt a fiftieth wedding anniversary renewal of vows.

Joshua is the son of the Reverend Julius del Pino, who was the pastor of the local Methodist Church in Pacific Palisades, California. In an era when it seemed rare for children to write letters, Joshua's thoughtful thank-you note and picture convey his "attitude of gratitude" and speak volumes about the way that his parents raised him. Joshua, like many young people from the community, enjoyed St. Matthew's Day Camp. The camp wasn't fancy, but our counselors were so devoted to the children that they made even the most basic activities special. I loved being involved in the camp and consider one of the greatest honors of my career to be the time when one of our counselors, Curt Massey,[37] and some of his cohorts tossed me unceremoniously—and to the delight of the entire camp—into the pool. I should add that this "baptism" occurred while I was still fully clothed in sport coat, shoes, and my clerical collar! I have long believed in the value of positive formative experiences for children during the long summer school holidays. The dividends of such a low-cost investment in our youth are so compelling that I would love to see summer camp be available for every child. Until the day when our government budget priorities shift—just imagine what even a fraction of the defense budget would translate into in terms of camp stipends—at least I can advocate for every congregation across America to provide camp scholarships for a few young people every year.

Joshua, I'm delighted that we could catch up recently. I wish you well. Keep up your good work with today's young people. Your friend, Peter Kreitler.

---

[37] Curt was one of my son Brad's best friends. He later became a Los Angeles police officer and, tragically, lost his life in the line of duty.

Thank you very much for the two tickets to the Dodger game. Thanks a lot! That was the best reason to come to church. I hope you enjoyed giving as much as I enjoyed receiving.

    Mac Clabaugh

Dear Father Peter,

Thank you very much for the two tickets to the Dodger game. I had a great time. The seats were five rows behind the Dodger dugout out in the lowest section. I could see the players' faces when they went into the dugout. You should of seen the smile on Guerrero's face when he hit his homer. Fernando pitched a great game. He gave up two runs on five hits. He also made one of the best reflex catches I have ever seen. In about the sixth or seventh inning, the batter hit a hard line-drive back up the middle. The ball was heading right at his head. He stuck out his glove and snagged it The Dodgers won the game 4–2. All of their runs came in the sixth inning. Dave Anderson led off with a bloop triple down the right field line. Steve Sax then doubled down the left field line to score Anderson. John Shelby then came within about one foot of hitting a home run. He hit the ball just above the 370 mark in left field. His double scored Sax. Guerrero then hit his home run about ten rows into the bleachers in left behind the 360 mark. Mike Marshall then doubled to left. Mickey Hatcher laid down a sacrifice bunt moving Marshall to third, but Phil Garner missed the ball on a suicide squeeze, and Marshall was caught in a rundown. The Reds' runs came in the second and I think the fourth innings. The first run came on Buddy Bell's solo homer, just to the left of the Dodger bullpen in left field. The Reds' second run came after Fernando struck out Reds pitcher Guy Hoffman. Then he walked Kal Daniels and Dave Concepcion doubled to left. Fernando then did not allow any more runs. The seats were some of the best I have ever had. The only other seats I had that I enjoyed as much were about three years ago. One game I was in the first row behind the Dodger dugout. The other time I was in the first row, aisle one, seat one, right behind home plate.

Thanks a lot! That was the best reason to come to church. I hope you enjoyed giving as much as I enjoyed receiving.

Sincerely,

Mac Clabaugh

Mac attended St. Matthew's parish and school, loves baseball, and comes from a great family. The last sentence of his descriptive letter brings a smile to my face every time I read it. No one has ever been so refreshingly forthright about why he or she enjoyed coming to church. Mac truly believed he received something tangible and reminded me that it is in giving that we are blessed. Mac blessed me with his play-by-play description of a sport that I loved to play as a young man and still follow to this day. Some of life's lessons come from the most surprising of places and his lesson is clear. His words, "That was the best reason to come to church. I hope you enjoyed giving as much as I enjoyed receiving" are priceless. Listen to our young people; from their mouths may come great truths.

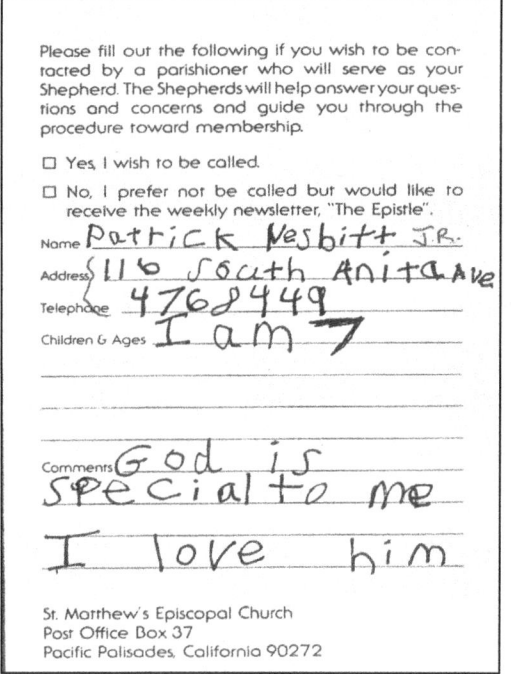

This is a response form that we placed in the pews at St. Matthew's. How marvelous and rare that a seven-year-old would fill out this kind of form on his own and with such a wonderful and personal comment! Even though I advocate for open dialogue with young people about religion and their understanding of God, I have yet to figure out when they actually begin to articulate their beliefs. My best guess is when they are around three to four years of age. One of the challenges for priests, rabbis, and ministers—the very people who, for many, are the key spokespersons for God—is figuring out how to make the Almighty understandable or relatable to young people. Here is how I attempted to explain God to three-to-five-year old children:

"Please hold up your hand; now blow on your hand. Do you see anything?"

"No," they would respond.

"Did you feel anything?"

"Yes," they would respond.

"That is how God is to many people. It is kind of a feeling—sort of like when you are going to sleep and Mom and Dad are not there with you, but you kind of feel they are near; that is like God for many people."

While my analogy was hardly the definitive explanation of God, my young audience could relate to it. Patrick's note reinforces my experience that early exposure may encourage the development of one's own personal understanding of a higher power or God—or not! Spoon-feeding a belief system, in my experience, usually backfires later in life, so instead I promote reading about and discussing all aspects of a spiritual or religious journey.

Dear Dad,

Went to the emergency room in St. Jhons [sic] hospital. Almost had operation for my ependic [sic]. Body is cloged [sic] (look below heart), took 3 ex-rays [sic], had blood test, heart rate test, and showed doctor Hutch my toe; he thought it was odd and once in a lifetime. Got the experience of a wheelchair and took off. Still have pains in my right side. Think I'll servive [sic]?

Still possible ependicidice [sic], taking the blood test (I almost died) hurt really badly and so did the ex-rays on the flat table. Got an extra ex-ray because we're studying the human body. Call me when you get home.

NUMBER

TO

CALL

123-4567

Mom sends her love too.

Laura lost her dad to cancer when she was just two years old. When her mother, Katy, and I were engaged to be married in 1985, I underwent a series of interviews and background checks to determine whether I was fit to serve as Laura's adopted father. We then met before the judge who would finalize the adoption. Part of the process involved five-year-old Laura choosing her new name. We, along with the judge, went over her options: Laura Hunt, Laura Kreitler, Laura Maurer Hunt, and Laura Maurer Hunt Kreitler. "What is your choice?" we asked. Laura asked, "I can choose any name?" We all agreed by nodding, and she responded in a loud clear voice, "I would like to be called Susan."

A couple of years later, Laura wrote me this note about her hospital experience. She continues to communicate with friends and family—minus the spelling errors of a precocious seven-year-old—on a regular basis and to surprise her parents with correspondence from the far-off places she explores as she balances her work with skiing. It is a real treat for us to get a glimpse of the globe through Laura's eyes. Thanks to the smartphone, she is able to share her travel with us through photos and videos as well as with her distinctive way of turning a phrase. I hope that Laura—indeed, everyone—will save the text of their digital communications along with the accompanying photos and mini movies so they can revisit them later, just as I do with my cherished letters.

Dear Peter,

Thanks for your kind note. Judge Jones is releasing me August 1! He must not have thought I was too guilty if he lets me out after [sixty] days of a three-year sentence! You would love this "country club," as 60 Minutes calls these camps. You bet! Ho! It is a cheap military-type barracks set in the middle of an Indiana field—absolutely no shade anywhere. It was built in 1963 to house 192 men; today there are 443 inmates. When I first arrived, I was in a room with twenty guys and then I got lucky?! I am now in permanent housing; [it's] one room 10' x 16' (measure that) with eight men and eight lockers—cozy? Now add to that a few broken screens, which means plenty of flies and no air conditioning in the entire complex and with these 100+ [degree] days and evenings—UGH! My roommates are really good guys. Diverse and lots of laughs. One must look at this as an experience and get through it with a sense of humor. I turned down running the print shop; I opted for landscaping and am in charge of the formal grounds in front of the camp. Just what I wanted? When I get out, I can hire myself out to stand around people at cocktail parties—where else can they get a real live felon who has done some "Down Time"? I can hardly wait to get on with the rest of my life. I feel I have made it through this with no scars but a great deal of new insight into life, my family, and friends!

Sincerely,

[Name Withheld]

Many of us have witnessed—especially recently—public figures being indicted and jailed, but usually those arrests are at arm's length. Other times, however, another's misfortune touches us personally. When a friend of mine was sentenced to jail, a bit of who I am was wounded as well. My good friend and his wonderful family were deeply affected by this event. I share this letter because we are called to stand with those we care about, especially during difficult times. Granted, the judge's sentence implies that the crime was not significant and the dramatically reduced jail time brought everyone a sigh of relief. This redacted account, taken from a hand-written, three-page letter, demonstrated to me the depth of my friend's character. I admire his compassion for others, his humor, and the journey of self-awareness that he underwent while he was incarcerated. I am impressed by my friend and his family's solidarity and the way they have collectively handled the whole ordeal. Since this incident, they have given back to their community and their church in many ways. I am reminded of the old adage that when the community of faith is at its best, it serves not as a hotel for saints, but as a hospital for sinners.

February 14, 1988

Valentine's Day,

Hola Pedro!

At long last it looks like you'll get to see these shows. I'm getting around to doing ½" VHS of both Ahimsa *and* Antarctica: The Last Continent, *the documentary I shot about a year ago.*

Work has been continuing—sporadic free-lance. I've started doing some things for the MacNeil-Lehrer News Hour. Also, on the horizon looms a major gig with Michael Tobias,[38] the producer I worked with on Ahimsa *and* Antarctica.

What's new with the Kreitlers? I keep hearing about the J. Paul Getty museum and photography. Are you still interacting with them? I gotta go. It's late and my mind's turning to mush. I hope you enjoy the shows.

   E

Stuart Keene, whom I nicknamed Enzo or "E," was a good friend. He was a member of my youth group in Kansas City, travelled to Mexico on our mission trips to work in rural villages, was my photography buddy, and visited us in California and Cape Cod. While we delight in newsy letters, like this one from "E," one of the hardest updates to receive is from a family member telling you that your cherished friend has died tragically and unexpectedly. Stuart was a professional cameraman and, while filming the Coors Classic Bike race in Colorado for ABC Sports, his camera platform collapsed. He fell to the ground and his large camera fell on his chest, killing him.

Ordination does not make us immune to tragedy, nor does it immediately vest us with all the skills necessary to process the loss of a family member or good friend. I do not think I will ever become numb to the tragedies of life. And rather than being out of place, a clergy person's tears or emotions over a loss reflect our humanity in a manner that words alone cannot express. My heart was broken, but my memory of him gives Stu everlasting life.

---

[38] Ironically, shortly thereafter I began working with author and filmmaker Michael Tobias on a television production.

December 28, 2009

To Palisadian-Post

This is in response to the condescending editorial by Peter Kreitler [that] the Post *published a couple of weeks ago in which he labeled those of us who don't agree with him about global warming "Flat Earthers." Peter is a pretty good guy, although he is very myopic about environmental issues. Peter, believe it or not, the earth heats or cools in less than 250,000-year cycles.*

I don't think there is anyone on the planet who doesn't believe we should have a healthy and clean environment, but whether or not global warming is entirely man-made or can be significantly influenced by man is up for debate...Mother Nature, for whatever cosmic reasons (sun spots, volcanoes, etc.) does her thing, and there is probably very little we can do about it, except be good citizens. So, Peter Kreitler can be as condescending and belligerent as he wants; in the long run, Mother Nature calls the shots.

Steven Miller, A Flat Earther

"Viewpoint – Climate Change or Climate Crisis" Palisadian-Post   *December 17, 2009*

...Contrary to the overly blatant, erroneous vitriol from the "flat earth" crowd....that is, the climate change skeptics...thousands of pure scientists from every reputable institution globally are reiterating the stringent warning of the Union of Concerned Scientists from 1992, summarized by visionary thinker Jacques Cousteau, "Unless we do something radical today, we will be unable to do anything at all tomorrow." For economic or political reasons, some wish to distort the truth, but the voices of reason will prevail as the overwhelming data will begin to trump all the dialogue in the future...Each of us can be the change we want to see in the world, and each step we take minimizes the chance of moving from climate change to climate crisis.

The above is an excerpt of the editorial I wrote in 2009 with which Steven took issue. The science tells us clearly that we are now in crisis mode. As for my friend Steven, all is well; he has come around to adopt a more reasoned approach to the subject. He too is a good guy.

P.S. I agree, Steven, Mother Nature needs help calling the shots. We all must do our part to help!

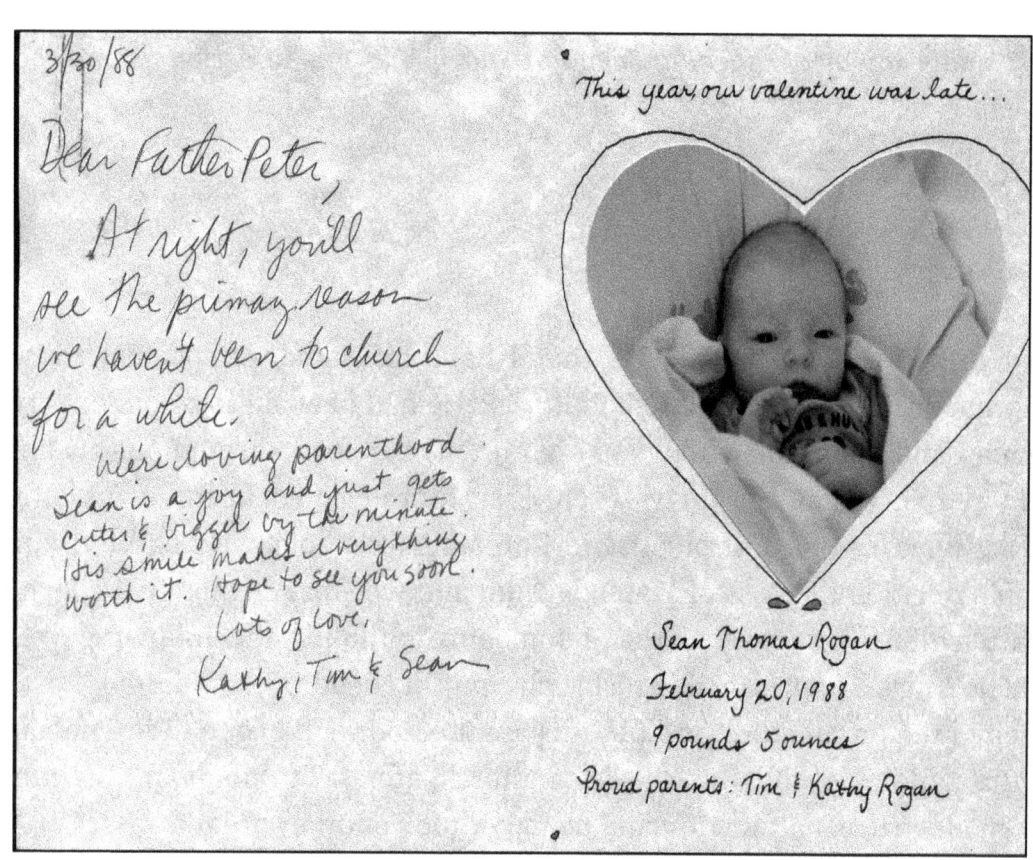

More than fair enough. Family first, folks!

Dear Peter,

I just want to reiterate what a nice service you gave for Rick. At such an emotional time for all of us, it was very comforting to have you there.

You always have a way of reaching deep into our hearts and affecting us in a special way. We miss you.

> *Love,*
>
> > *Jill*

The most difficult memorial service that I have officiated, other than those for my parents, was for my good friend Rick Philbrick. He had been an Olympic-quality skier as a young man and maintained a love of high-intensity sports throughout his life. He was always in shape, yet at age forty-seven, Rick literally died in my arms after having finished a game of squash at our friend Rob Maguire's house. He had felt faint, so we stopped playing. I got a glass of water for him and we were sitting on a couch catching our breath when he suggested that I join him for lunch the following Wednesday. Suddenly he blurted out, "Oh, my gosh!" and put his head back and died. I grabbed the phone, called the paramedics, and put Rick on the floor and began CPR. The paramedics applied the paddles of life about seven minutes later, all to no avail. Rick's heart had suffered an electrical malfunction and he never took another breath.

The church was packed for his service. When I told the story of his last words inviting me to lunch, I stressed the importance of reciprocity, of both friends making the effort to stay in regular contact. That powerful event underscored that each day we have is a gift. This unexpected, but gratefully received, note of appreciation is an example of what Rev. Coleman meant when he told me back in 1963 in India—"do not look for rewards, but they will come, Peter."

Dear Peter,

In the past couple of weeks, I have heard...that there has been some disquiet within the Episcopal community over the fact that Pamela and I were married in your church. I am saddened for any discomfort this may have caused you, particularly [since] you have given so much to Pamela and to me. Having been turned down repeatedly and for many months by Roman Catholic priests, most of who were close friends, your offer to minister to our love moved us very deeply. In fact, it inspired us to understand more intimately the gentleness and wisdom of Christ, who knows the greatest revelation of God is love. I say this to you not out of sentiment, of that blindness that sometimes comes with emotional exhilaration; rather, I say this to you as a brother priest who is convinced that the Spirit of God is not found in man-made laws [that] forbid marital love to priests. The Spirit of God is found in priests who welcome strangers, who heal hearts broken or rejected, who listen to the spirit of truth rather than to the letter of the law. All of these things you manifested to us when we first came to your church; that is why tears welled in Pamela's eyes. After more than ten years of research and prayer concerning the historical origins of the laws mandating celibacy for priest in the Latin Rite, I now realize that the mandatory aspect of celibacy is contrary to human nature, to God's will, and to the good of the church. It will take time for Rome to realize this truth, and it would be much easier for me to simply walk away from the deaf ears within my own tradition. But, as you know, I feel God wants me to address this wrong that is killing the Roman Catholic priesthood. You reached out to us at an extremely important time in our lives. Your listening helped Pamela to trust again that priestly ministry...can nurture love and deeper union with Christ. Your baptizing her occasioned profound joy. And it was evident to everyone who attended the marriage Eucharist that love was present, that faith was real. For these graces we are deeply grateful to Bishop Corrigan, to Greg, and especially to you.   Sincerely, Terry

Personal, powerful, and prophetic, these words flow from one of the most respected Roman Catholic priests that I have known. When Episcopal clergy are asked to celebrate the sacrament of marriage, the law requires that we ask three questions: Are you blood relatives? Have either of you been judged insane by a court of law? Are you currently married to someone else? If the answer to all three questions is negative, and if either the bride or the groom has been baptized, then we are good to go in The Episcopal Church. I agreed to perform Pam and Terry's wedding, contingent on them meeting my requirement of at least five hours of premarital counseling. Their love story and the larger issue of whether Roman Catholic priests should be allowed to marry and to retain their standing in the church are the subjects of their book *What God Hath Joined*. I am proud of my role in their story.

United States District Court

Warren W. Eginton, Sr., District Judge

My dear Reverend Canon,   *June 12, 2011*

I write, along with I suspect many others in your audience, to express my awe at your forensic power. You must leave your congregation awed and delighted every time you ascend the rostrum to sermonize. Your family must live in a constant atmosphere of appreciation of your talent. Do they film your performances to preserve them for posterity? For me, the most impressive aspect of your presentation is that it was done without a single note, not even a scribble on the cuff. Obama is considered to be a most impressive off-the-cuff speaker, but...he had the advantage of a teleprompter, as most presidents are wont to use. You were bereft of any such aide and yet easily equaled his best performances. Thank you for an entertaining and rewarding half hour. I would be happy to join [your congregation] but I am wedded to the unattractive East Coast because we are happily immunized from your eternal mudslides, fires, and earthquakes. Dull life here, but at least our insurance rates are lower, and we can hope to avoid an unexpected end at the hands of a relentless Mother Nature. Thanks, and best to you and your fiftieth reunion class. Hope that you enjoyed your weekend as much as we enjoyed our seventieth. [I'm just] happy to be able to arrive at that point in time.

Sincerely, Warren Eginton '41

If I were ever on trial, I'd want Judge Eginton behind the bench. His humor and his exaggerated praise of the sermon I gave during alumni weekend at the Loomis School make this letter one of my favorites from my "shoebox." If I had to choose between Judge Eginton being my mentor or being my surrogate grandfather, I would ask for both as he shares their wonderful traits of humor, wisdom, and support. I can relate to his comment that he was just "happy to be able to arrive at that point in time." I thought making it to my fiftieth was special enough! We were both grateful that we were able to connect with our remaining classmates at the school where our learning began in earnest. I had never met Judge Eginton before but, like the Good Samaritan who gave of himself to a complete stranger, he gave me a powerful, enduring gift of affirmation and appreciation. Tweets, texts, and email are more immediate ways to communicate, but are also more ephemeral. A personal letter, even to a stranger, has the potential to transform and embolden. Thanks, Warren, you represent the best of any Connecticut Yankee I know.

P.S. I was born in Middletown, Connecticut.

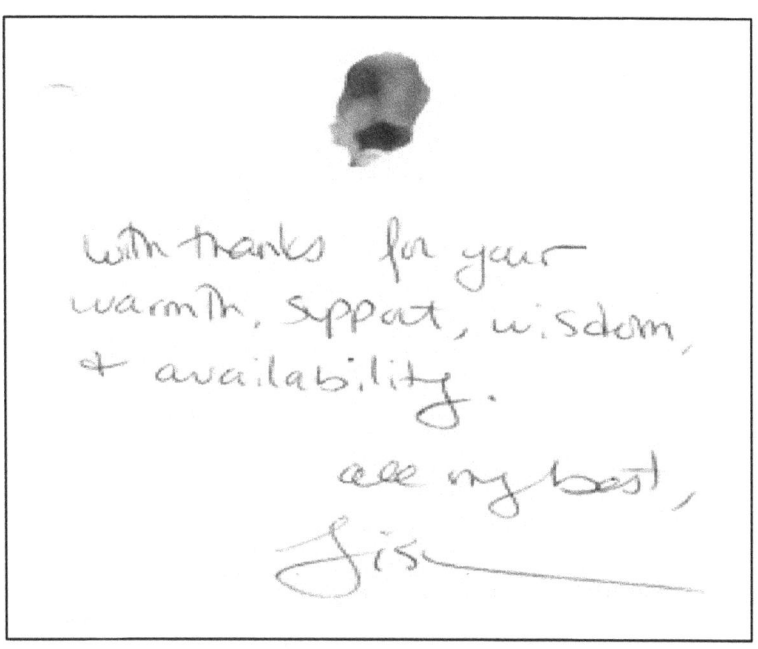

Retirement arrives at our doorsteps all too quickly and we're advised to start preparing for its eventuality early on. Most people think of preparing financially for retirement, but it is equally important to map out the life you want to live. How will you remain engaged in the pursuits that you find meaningful? To their credit, many clergy continue to serve the church, community, or nation in some capacity long after they reach retirement age.[39] The frequency with which we perform sacramental functions—the baptizing, marrying, and burying that keep us so busy during our careers—may diminish in retirement, but we must never stop caring for all of creation. Even when we are well into our nineties, we can find ways to use our skills in the service of the greater good.

One night over dinner, some friends asked me whether I still counseled. I told them that I do in those instances in which, following an intake interview, I feel I can be of help. They then told me that they had a young friend who might benefit from my advice. My friends arranged an initial conversation for me with Lisa. She impressed me with her sincerity, intellect, and integrity, and we decided to continue our long-distance dialogue. Her note validates much of what I learned in seminary about being a priest. My teachers used to remind me to be open to the wisdom of others because doing so enables them to be receptive to yours. "Peter, you have two ears and one mouth. Listen twice as much as you speak," was the advice offered in one of my pastoral care courses. In retirement, our time is not as scheduled as it was during our careers, so there really is no excuse not to be available when we are needed. The bottom line may be this: clergy never really retire.

---

[39]Canon law of The Episcopal Church stipulates mandatory retirement from full-time service at age seventy-two.

Nov. 1, 2018

Dear Father Peter,

What a read...

Teary in some places...Laughing in others...

...and almost fifty years—what a tribute to you and to all those you touched.

Hugs and love from one of your oldest (?) buddies—and here we are! How many years later?

Nelle

Our complex and transient lifestyles make it tough to sustain friendships over many years, but what a cherished gift it is when they do pass the test of time. I have known Nelle for seven decades. We are the same age and our grandparents lived down the street from each other. Today our extended families continue to share summers on Cape Cod. What a blessing!

It was only natural that Nelle should read a draft manuscript for this book, and her note touched me deeply. I suppose the universal lesson learned is that deep, long-lasting friendships are especially important to clergy of all faiths because we often have "thousands of acquaintances," yet only a few close friends. As we age and lose those close to us, each new year is time to acknowledge and appreciate our special relationships. Stories told, memories shared, and pictures on the wall keep the good friends up close and personal. Amen!

December 1984

May the peace, love, and awe of your moments of being reflect and radiate on Earth's humankind.

Tom Brod

Dr. Tom is a renowned psychodynamic psychiatrist. And while I don't know him terribly well, he has always exhibited a level of serenity usually associated with practitioners of an intense spiritual discipline.

I have spent time at Well Spring in Germantown, Maryland in an extensive silent retreat as well as two weeks at St. Benedict's, a Trappist monastery in Snow Mass, Colorado. I have also led retreats at Mt. Calvary monastery in Santa Barbara, California. Monks have a demeanor I wish I could emulate more often. I have learned that nothing seems to faze people who detach from the material world. Dr. Tom is the exceptional person who exudes the type of inner strength practiced in the monastic community, even in the middle of the sprawling, fast-paced metropolis of Los Angeles.

Spiritual disciplines take many forms and shapes, and today's clergy would be well served by a habitual practice of prayer or meditation. Thank you, Tom, for personally modeling such an admirable behavior trait and for sharing this beautiful sentiment—it is so reflective of who you are!

Dependable friends, like the sender of this card, are welcome constants in an unpredictable world. Imagine one of your wedding guests caring enough to send you a card every year to memorialize your special day. A former member of my youth group in Kansas City does just that. Don Hall Jr. is the "Don" who, along with his wife, signed and sent this anniversary card, just as he has done ever since 1985. Katy and I also receive Christmas cards from the Hall family every year. I can't imagine anyone in our country—other than, possibly, the president—who sends out more greeting cards than Don. Then again, he comes by the practice naturally. In 1910 his paternal grandfather, Joyce Hall, started a small greeting card company in Kansas City, Missouri. He called it Hallmark.

The few moments it takes to send a card to mark a special occasion is a high impact way of letting people know you are thinking about them. None of us are too busy to adopt this thoughtful habit.

P.S. Remember I told you that I had stored these *Dear Father Peter* letters in shoeboxes for safekeeping? The Hallmark website notes that Joyce Hall stepped off the train in Kansas City with nothing but two shoeboxes of postcards under his arm. The moral of the story is do not throw away your shoeboxes!

3/28/87

Father Peter,

Apology accepted.

Viola

This last note is all about taking responsibility, apologizing, and forgiveness. The author had been upset at something I had said or done and I wrote an apology, which she accepted.

Please let me extend an apology to anyone I may have offended throughout my career. I am deeply sorry if, because of me, you harbor resentment, or feel displeasure towards the church or God. As every public figure knows, our words—whether a simple phrase, off-hand comment, or a full-blown diatribe against some injustice—may trigger a response of anger, disgust, or deep disappointment. I am sorry if my behavior or words offended.

I have always viewed myself as a fallible human being first, husband second, father third, friend fourth, and priest fifth. I have made mistakes in all categories during my life. At the end of my days, I hope I will be remembered as one whose belief and behavior lined up. I was taught in seminary to be faithful, because no one among us can be successful all the time, and no one is perfect. Perhaps you perceived my life differently. Please accept my apologies and pass your blessing of forgiveness on me, as Viola did so long ago.

A picture is worth a thousand words.
   English language adage

It is often said that a single picture is worth a thousand words. I have chosen four photographs taken of me that, perhaps more than any other images, define my ministry as well as my hope for the future.

This first image encapsulates my twenty years in parish work from 1970-1990. The sacerdotal functions of a priest are sacred, and baptism—the rite that welcomes one into the Christian community—is one sacrament that always made me smile. Children do have a wonderful way of stealing the show. I learned early in my career not to have any behavioral expectations of them because surprises always awaited me. In this picture, I am baptizing Lydia and Charlton Heston's grandson Jack. I am reading from the Book of Common Prayer and, to my delight, little Jack's eyes are transfixed as though he is paying rapt attention. This illustrative photograph, taken by Lydia, emphasizes the significance of the family rituals that define, in part, the structure of communities of faith worldwide. Reflecting upon an almost five-decade career in the priesthood, there is no greater privilege than working with young people. There was no aspect of ministry that I took more seriously than working with children, from the very young to young adults. I led chapel every Monday for preschoolers and offered a daily chapel for kindergarteners to eighth-graders, addressed grandchildren at funerals, and created sermons that young people could relate to. I was proud to have been called "The Pied Piper of Children." Young people have been inspirations and teachers for me. Indeed, Mrs. Heston's remarkable portrait of a pivotal moment in the life of Jack Heston is worth a thousand words.

The second picture, taken in urban Los Angeles, appeared in the April 1995 issue of *National Geographic*, which paid tribute to the twenty-fifth anniversary of Earth Day. The *National Geographic* retrospective of the environmental movement opened with, "Nationwide street demonstrations in 1970 helped turn Americans 'green.' Here are seven of the dedicated millions whose commitment is bearing fruit." National Geographic photographer Randy Olson, who lived with Katy and me for a week, captured this photo of me lying in the gutter, explaining to two attentive passersby how storm drains bring urban waste to the ocean. In the background, members of the non-profit organization Human Efforts at Vitalizing Youth are removing graffiti, a blight that touches every corner of the planet and another visual reminder of our fragile island home's degradation at the hands of humans. Randy clicked the shutter over twenty-three hundred times, and, ironically, the editors selected the one image that mimics the position that a priest takes during his or her ordination.

My pastoral and sacerdotal ministries have never stopped completely, but since 1991 the majority of my time and energy has been dedicated to environmental issues. This *National Geographic* photo clearly represents that focus. I will never stop lending my voice to the voiceless and working to preserve this remarkable home we have inherited because a livable and sustainable planet is essential for a healthy quality of life for all. I will be bold enough to proclaim that we are facing the most important theological issue in the history of the human race. The preservation of God's creation should and will be the final uniting force of all peoples on the earth.

The third picture worth a thousand words was taken at St. Matthew's Church when the 22nd Presiding Bishop of The Episcopal Church, John Hines, came to speak. I got to know the "P.B." when I was in seminary because my good friend and fellow member of the basketball team John Hines introduced me to his dad. Bishop Hines loved basketball and invited several of the team members to stay in his apartment when we played General Seminary in New York City. A strong voice for the marginalized in our society, Bishop Hines' prophetic voice through the turbulent times of the 1960s—my college and seminary years—and during my early years as a priest, continues to inform my theology and worldview to this day.

My teachers, mentors, and role models have been: Rev. Charles Baldwin, Al Beebe, Ed Begley Jr., Father Thomas Berry, Rt. Rev. Frederick Borsch, David Brower, Bill Bruns, Rt. Rev. John Bruno, Rev. Dr. Dick Busch, Dr. John Cobb, Rev. Ken Coleman, Frank Davis, Coach Ralph Erickson, Stanley Sessions Gwillim, David Hall, Rev. John Harper, Rt. Rev. John E. Hines, Very Rev. Martha Horne, Robert Johnson, John and "Billie" Kreitler, Nanny and Poppy Kreitler, Ann and "Bill" Lucas, Very Rev. Ian Markham, PhD, Dr. John O'Hearne, Alexandra Paul, John Quigley, Dr. John Seeley, Attosa Soltani, and Very Rev. Jesse Trotter.

Regardless of what we choose to do in life, the bonds of brotherhood and sisterhood that we form along the way can be one of the most rewarding aspects of our careers. Several years ago, the movie *Three Amigos,* featuring Chevy Chase, Steve Martin, and Martin Short, was a popular hit. This final photograph is from 1969 and features me playing wall ball with three of my favorite amigos at VTS one afternoon after class. Yours truly is on the left; Pittman McGehee, former dean of Christ Church Cathedral in Houston, eminent Jungian counselor, and author and lecturer, is to my left, followed by parish priest, progressive educator, and innovative interim minister, John M. Hines (wearing his favorite hat), and George Andrews, former headmaster of St. Georges School in Rhode Island and St. Andrew's School in Boca Raton, Florida. Here we have four members of the infamous VTS '69 basketball team and four individuals who chose distinctly different paths to exercise their ministries—an environmental focus for Kreitler, a counseling emphasis for McGehee, a parish ministry for Hines, and an educational career for Andrews. There are other paths to be chosen, but we four have had rich and rewarding lives serving God and God's church for a collective two hundred years of ministry since we graduated from seminary.

Acknowledgments

Johannes Gutenberg's printing press with moveable type and his 1454 Bible brought printing to the West and democratized the distribution of knowledge forever. The Church of England renounced Papal Authority in 1534 and the resulting Anglicanism is based on faith, tradition, and reason. The King James Version of the Bible was written in 1611. The Protestant Episcopal Church in the United States of America was founded in 1789. In 1823, the Diocese of Virginia established Virginia Theological Seminary (VTS), the second Episcopal seminary in the United States. These are the historical underpinnings of my ministry—the ministry that I have tried to capture in *Dear Father Peter*.

I am thankful for

> The instructors at the Loomis School, Brown University, and VTS, who taught me how to think. My lifelong teachers have also been the young and old alike who wrote to me during my career.
>
> Lee Adinolfi, Michelle Bohan, Suzanne Flynn, and Nelle Huettig, who read drafts of *Dear Father Peter*; and Joe and Cindy Connolly for listening incessantly to tales about the on-going development of the book.
>
> Jimmy "Bart" Bartholomew and Robert Tebbe, who provided technical assistance with scanning and photography.
>
> Linda Dienno, Barney Hawkins, and Ian Markham from VTS, who encouraged and shepherded the publication of *Dear Father Peter*.
>
> Dorothy Pearson of VTS Press for her patience as I kept adding new letters that I discovered in old files and folders, her editorial expertise, her push to clarify my commentary when it was obtuse or obfuscating the meaning I was trying to convey, and her "wordsmithing." I will be forever grateful for her thoughtful listening and conscientious research. *Dear Father Peter* has been a fun project to share with Dorothy.

And finally, I am eternally thankful for Katy, who enabled me to focus on *Dear Father Peter* with the level of intensity required for two years of writing following two years of discernment as I read over fifteen hundred letters. She has been by my side as Nurse Nightingale and caring critic simultaneously; her presence, love, and encouragement have been the bedrock of my career. "No man is an island unto himself," to quote the famous Anglican cleric John Donne, and this author is indebted to Katy for sharing my journey for almost four decades.

Further Reading

Berry, Thomas. n.d. *Dream of the Earth.* San Francisco: Sierra Club.

Cobb, John B. Jr. 1972. *Is it Too Late?: A Theology of Ecology.* New York: Benzinger Bruce and Glencoe, Inc.

Cobb, John B. Jr., and Herman Daly. 1989. *For the Common Good: Redirecting the Economy Toward Community, the Environment, and a Sustainable Future.* Boston: Beacon Press.

Johnson, Robert. 1989. *He: Understanding Masculine Psychology.* New York: Harper Perennial.

—. 1989. *She: Understanding Feminine Psychology.* New York: Harper Perennial.

—. 1983. *We: Understanding the Psychology of Romantic Love.* San Francisco: HarperSanFrancisco.

Jones, Richard J., and J. Barney Hawkins IV, eds. 2010. *Staying One, Remaining Open: Educating Leaders for a 21st-Century Church.* New York: Morehouse Publishing

Kreitler, Peter. 1991. *Flatiron: A Photographic History of the World's First Steel Frame Skyscraper, 1901-1990.* Aia Press.

—. 2001. *United We Stand: Flying the American Flag.* Diane Publishing Company.

Kreitler, Peter, and Bill Bruns. 1981. *Affair Prevention.* New York: Macmillan.

Ruiz, Don Miguel. 1997. *The Four Agreements: A Practical Guide to Personal Freedom (A Toltec Wisdom Book).* San Rafael: Amber-Allen Publishing .

Straub, Gerard Thomas. 1986. *Salvation for Sale: An Insider's View of Pat Robertson.* Buffalo: Prometheus Books.

Sweeney, Pamela Shoop, and Terrance Sweeney. 1993. *What God Hath Joined: The Real-Life Love Story that Shook the Catholic Church.* New York: Ballantine Books.

U.S. Department of Housing and Urban Development. n.d. *United States Interagency Council on Homelessness.* Accessed May 2, 2019. https://www.usich.gov/homelessness-statistics/ca/.

This anonymous (or so I thought on my first reading) note appeared tucked under the wiper blade on the windshield of my car. Dorothy Pearson and I had just finished an editing session of *Dear Father Peter* and were done for the day. We thought a passerby was interested in my car, but then I noticed the long acronym at the bottom. In the coded language of endearment that my wife and I share, "TTB" stands for "The Tall Blond." Mystery author's identity revealed! Katy's note is one last piece of special correspondence I would like to share that punctuates the value of handwritten communication.

www.ingramcontent.com/pod-product-compliance
Lightning Source LLC
Chambersburg PA
CBHW080540170426
43195CB00016B/2629